Just The

facts101

Textbook Key Facts

Textbook Outlines, Highlights, and Practice Quizzes

Comparing Religions: Coming to Terms

by Jeffrey J. Kripal, 1st Edition

Title Page

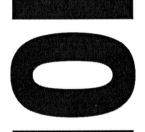

facts101
LEARNING SYSTEM

"Just the Facts101" is a Content Technologies publication and tool designed to give you all the facts from your textbooks. Visit JustTheFacts101.com for the full practice test for each of your chapters for virtually any of your textbooks.

Facts101 has built custom study tools specific to your textbook. We provide all of the factual testable information and unlike traditional study guides, we will never send you back to your textbook for more information.

YOU WILL NEVER HAVE TO HIGHLIGHT A BOOK AGAIN!

Facts101 StudyGuides
All of the information in this StudyGuide is written specifically for your textbook. We include the key terms, places, people, and concepts... the information you can expect on your next exam!

Want to take a practice test?
Throughout each chapter of this StudyGuide you will find links to JustTheFacts101.com where you can select specific chapters to take a complete test on, or you can subscribe and get practice tests for up to 12 of your textbooks, along with other exclusive Jtf101.com tools like problem solving labs and reference libraries.

JustTheFacts101.com
Only Jtf101.com gives you the outlines, highlights, and PRACTICE TESTS specific to your textbook. JustTheFacts101.com is an online application where you'll discover study tools designed to make the most of your limited study time.

By purchasing this book, you get 50% off the normal monthly subscription fee!. Just enter the promotional code **'DK73DW24582'** on the Jtf101.com registration screen.

www.JustTheFacts101.com

ISBN(s): 9781490299464. PUBI-6.201469

Comparing Religions: Coming to Terms
Jeffrey J. Kripal, 1st

CONTENTS

1. Comparative Practices in Global History: If Horses Had Hands

CHAPTER OUTLINE: KEY TERMS, PEOPLE, PLACES, CONCEPTS

_____ | Ramana Maharshi

_____ | Charles Robert Darwin

_____ | Religious studies

_____ | Persecution

_____ | Guru

_____ | Nanak

_____ | Mysticism

_____ | Philosophical analysis

_____ | Polytheism

_____ | Axial Age

_____ | Herodotus

_____ | Xenophanes

_____ | Anthropomorphism

_____ | Plotinus

_____ | Orientalism

_____ | Plato

_____ | Theology

_____ | CoSMoS

_____ | Monotheism

_____ | Panentheism

_____ | Pantheism

1. Comparative Practices in Global History: If Horses Had Hands

Religious experience

Election

Ernst Bergmann

Torah

Renaissance

Apologetics

Authority

Heterodoxy

Orthodoxy

Polemic

Aristotle

Hippo

Metaphysics

Quran

Demon

Albert Schweitzer

Salvation

Neoplatonism

Criticism

Historical criticism

Logos

1. Comparative Practices in Global History: If Horses Had Hands

CHAPTER OUTLINE: KEY TERMS, PEOPLE, PLACES, CONCEPTS

	Metaphor
	Magi
	Revelation
	Manichaeism
	Dualism
	Sharia
	Attitude
	Violence
	I Ching
	Iconoclasm
	Sufi
	Advaita Vedanta
	Upanishads
	Caste
	Colonialism
	Purity
	Theory
	Dalit
	KabÄ«r
	Purana
	Sikhism

1. Comparative Practices in Global History: If Horses Had Hands

_____	Buddha
_____	Buddhism
_____	Confucianism
_____	Confucius
_____	Daoism

CHAPTER HIGHLIGHTS & NOTES: KEY TERMS, PEOPLE, PLACES, CONCEPTS

Ramana Maharshi	Sri Ramana Maharshi (December 30, 1879 - April 14, 1950), born Venkataraman Iyer, was a Hindu spiritual master ('jnani'). He was born to a Tamil-speaking Brahmin family in Tiruchuzhi, Tamil Nadu. After experiencing at age 16 what he later described as liberation (moksha), he left home for Arunachala, a mountain considered sacred by Hindus.
Charles Robert Darwin	Charles Robert Darwin FRS (12 February 1809 - 19 April 1882) was an English naturalist who established that all species of life have descended over time from common ancestors, and proposed the scientific theory that this branching pattern of evolution resulted from a process that he called natural selection. He published his theory with compelling evidence for evolution in his 1859 book On the Origin of Species. The scientific community and much of the general public came to accept evolution as a fact in his lifetime, but it was not until the emergence of the modern evolutionary synthesis from the 1930s to the 1950s that a broad consensus developed that natural selection was the basic mechanism of evolution.
Religious studies	File:Religious syms.svg Religious studies is the academic field of multi-disciplinary, secular study of religious beliefs, behaviors, and institutions. It describes, compares, interprets, and explains religion, emphasising systematic, historically-based, and cross-cultural perspectives. While theology attempts to understand the intentions of a supernatural force (such as deities), religious studies tries to study human religious behavior and belief from outside any particular religious viewpoint.
Persecution	Persecution is the systematic mistreatment of an individual or group by another group. The most common forms are religious persecution, ethnic persecution, and political persecution, though there is naturally some overlap between these terms.

Guru	A Guru is one who is regarded as having great knowledge, wisdom and authority in a certain area, and who uses it to guide others . As a principle for the development of consciousness it leads the creation from unreality to reality, from the darkness of ignorance to the light of knowledge. In its purest form this principle manifests on earth as a divine incarnation (saint), a person with supreme knowledge about God and all creation.
Nanak	Guru Nanak Dev Ji (Punjabi: à¨—à©à¨°à©, à¨¨à¾à¨¨à• à¨¦à©‡à¨µ, Hindi: à¤—à¥à¤°à¥ à¤¨à¾à¤¨à• à¤¦à¥‡à¤µ, Urdu: Ú¯Ø±Ù^Ù†Ø§Ù†Ú© Guru NÄnak) (15 April 1469 -22 September 1539) is the first of the ten Sikh Gurus. Sikhs believe that all subsequent Gurus possessed Guru Nanak's divinity and religious authority. Guru Nanak Dev Ji was born on 20 October 1469, now celebrated as Prakash Divas of Guru Nanak, into the Bedi Kshatriya family (a prominent Hindu community of Punjab), in the village of RÄi BhÅi dÄ« TalwandÄ«, now called Nankana Sahib, near Lahore, Pakistan.
Mysticism	Mysticism is the pursuit of communion with, identity with divinity, spiritual truth intuition, instinct or insight. Mysticism usually centers on a practice or practices intended to nurture those experiences or awareness. Mysticism may be dualistic, maintaining a distinction between the self and the divine, or may be nondualistic.
Philosophical analysis	Philosophical analysis is a general term for techniques typically used by philosophers in the analytic tradition that involve 'breaking down' (i.e. analyzing) philosophical issues.
Polytheism	Polytheism is the belief in and worship of multiple deities, called gods and goddesses. These are usually assembled into a pantheon, along with their own mythologies and rituals. Many religions, both historical and contemporary, have a belief in Polytheism, such as Hinduism, Buddhism, Shinto, Ancient Greek Polytheism, Roman Polytheism, Germanic Polytheism, Slavic Polytheism, Chinese folk religion, Neopagan faiths and Anglo-Saxon paganism.
Axial Age	Axial Age or Axial Period (Ger. Achsenzeit, 'axis time') is a term coined by German philosopher Karl Jaspers to describe the period from 800 to 200 BC, during which, according to Jaspers, similar revolutionary thinking appeared in India, China and the Occident. The period is also sometimes referred to as the Axis Age.
Herodotus	Herodotus of Halicarnassus was a Greek historian who lived in the 5th century BC . He is regarded as the 'Father of History' in Western culture. He was the first historian known to collect his materials systematically, test their accuracy to a certain extent and arrange them in a well-constructed and vivid narrative.
Xenophanes	Xenophanes of Colophon was a Greek philosopher, theologian, poet, and social and religious critic. Knowledge of his views comes from fragments of his poetry, surviving as quotations by later Greek writers.

1. Comparative Practices in Global History: If Horses Had Hands

Anthropomorphism	Anthropomorphism is the attribution of human characteristics to non-human creatures and beings, phenomena, material states and objects or abstract concepts. Examples include animals and plants depicted as creatures with human motivation able to reason and converse and forces of nature such as winds, rain or the sun. The term derives from the combination of the Greek á¼„νθρωπος , 'human' and μορφÎ® (morphÄ"), 'shape' or 'form'.
Plotinus	Plotinus was a major philosopher of the ancient world. In his system of theory there are the three principles: the One, the Intellect, and the Soul. His teacher was Ammonius Saccas and he is of the Platonic tradition.
Orientalism	Orientalism is a term used by art historians, literary and cultural studies scholars for the imitation or depiction of aspects of Middle Eastern, and East Asian cultures (Eastern cultures) by American and European writers, designers and artists. In particular, Orientalist painting, depicting more specifically 'the Middle East', was one of the many specialisms of 19th century Academic art. Since the publication of Edward Said's Orientalism, the term has arguably acquired a negative connotation.
Plato	Plato was a Classical Greek philosopher, mathematician, student of Socrates, writer of philosophical dialogues, and founder of the Academy in Athens, the first institution of higher learning in the Western world. Along with his mentor, Socrates, and his student, Aristotle, Plato helped to lay the foundations of Western philosophy and science. In the words of A. N. Whitehead:' The safest general characterization of the European philosophical tradition is that it consists of a series of footnotes to Plato.'
Theology	Theology is the rational and systematic study of religion and its influences and of the nature of religious truth, or the learned profession acquired by specialized courses in religion, usually taught at a college or seminary. Augustine of Hippo defined the Latin equivalent, theologia, as 'reasoning or discussion concerning the Deity'; Richard Hooker defined 'theology' in English as 'the science of things divine'. The term can, however, be used for a variety of different disciplines or forms of discourse.
CoSMoS	CoSMoS is a UK funded research project seeking do build capacity in generic modelling tools and simulation techniques for complex systems. Its acronym stands for Complex Systems Modelling and Simulation. This is a four-year project, running from 2007 to 2011 as a collaboration between the University of York and Kent, with further collaborations from the University of Abertay Dundee and Bristol Robotics Laboratory.
Monotheism	Monotheism is the belief in the existence of one god, as distinguished from polytheism, the belief in more than one god, and atheism, the absence of belief in any god or gods.

	Monotheism is characteristic of the Abrahamic religions, (Judaism, Christianity, Islam and Baha'i Faith), but is also present in Neoplatonism and in Sikhism and it is difficult to delineate from notions such as pantheism and monism.

Ostensibly monotheistic religions may still include concepts of a plurality of the divine; for example, the Trinity, in which God is one being in three eternal persons (the Father, the Son and the Holy Spirit). |
| Panentheism | Panentheism (from Greek π?v (pân) 'all'; ?v (en) 'in'; and θε?ς (theós) 'God'; 'all-in-God') is a belief system which posits that the divine exists (be it a monotheistic God, polytheistic gods, or an eternal cosmic animating force), interpenetrates every part of nature and timelessly extends beyond it. Panentheism differentiates itself from pantheism, which holds that the divine is synonymous with the universe.

In panentheism, the universe in the first formulation is practically the whole itself. |
Pantheism	Pantheism is the view that the Universe and God are identical. Pantheists thus do not believe in a personal, or anthropomorphic god. The word derives from the Greek (pan) meaning 'all' and the Greek (theos) meaning 'God'.
Religious experience	A religious experience is a subjective experience in which an individual reports contact with a transcendent reality, an encounter or union with the divine. Such an experience often involves arriving at some knowledge or insight previously unavailable to the subject yet unnaccountable or unforseeable according to the usual conceptual or psychological framework within which the subject has been used to operating. Religious experience generally brings understanding, partial or complete, of issues of a fundamental character that may have been a cause (whether consciously ackowledged or not) of anguish or alienation to the subject for an extended period of time.
Election	An election is a formal decision-making process by which a population chooses an individual to hold public office. Elections have been the usual mechanism by which modern representative democracy has operated since the 17th century. Elections may fill offices in the legislature, sometimes in the executive and judiciary, and for regional and local government.
Ernst Bergmann	Ernst Bergmann (7 August 1881, Colditz, Kingdom of Saxony - 16 April 1945, Naumburg) was a German philosopher and proponent of Nazism.

He studied philosophy and German philology at the University of Leipzig and got his PhD in 1905. Subsequently he continued his studies in Berlin. Later he returned to Leipzig, where he received the status of Privatdozent at the university in 1911. In 1916 he was awarded the position of Ausserordentlicher Professor (professor without chair). |

1. Comparative Practices in Global History: If Horses Had Hands

Torah	The term 'Torah' , refers either to the Five Books of Moses or to the entirety of Judaism's founding legal and ethical religious texts. A 'Sefer Torah' (×¡Öµ×¤Ö¶¨×¨ ×ªÖ¼×•Ö¹×·Ö¸×", 'book of Torah') or Torah scroll, is a copy of the Torah written on parchment in a formal, traditional manner by a specially trained scribe under very strict requirements. The Torah is the first of three parts of the Tanakh , the founding religious document of Judaism, Messiannic, and Hebrew belief, and is divided into five books, whose names in English are Genesis, Exodus, Leviticus, Numbers, and Deuteronomy, in reference to their themes .
Renaissance	The Renaissance was a cultural movement that spanned the period roughly from the 14th to the 17th century, beginning in Italy in the Late Middle Ages and later spreading to the rest of Europe. Though the invention of printing sped the dissemination of ideas from the later 15th century, the changes of the Renaissance were not uniformly experienced across Europe. As a cultural movement, it encompassed innovative flowering of Latin and vernacular literatures, beginning with the 14th-century resurgence of learning based on classical sources, which contemporaries credited to Petrarch, the development of linear perspective and other techniques of rendering a more natural reality in painting, and gradual but widespread educational reform.
Apologetics	Apologetics is the discipline of defending a position (often religious) through the systematic use of information. Early Christian writers (c. 120-220) who defended their faith against critics and recommended their faith to outsiders were called apologists. The term apologetics etymologically derives from the Classical Greek word apologia.
Authority	Authority is the legitimate or socially approved use of power. It is the legitimate power which one person or a group holds over another. The element of legitimacy is vital to the notion of authority and is the main means by which authority is distinguished from the more general concept of power.
Heterodoxy	Heterodoxy in a religious sense means 'any opinions or doctrines at variance with an official or orthodox position'. Under this definition, heterodoxy is similar to unorthodoxy, while the adjective 'heterodox' could be applied to a dissident. Heterodoxy is also an ecclesiastical term of art, defined in various ways by different religions and churches.
Orthodoxy	The word orthodox, from Greek orthos ('right', 'true', 'straight') + doxa ('opinion' or 'belief', related to dokein, 'to think'), is generally used to mean the adherence to accepted norms, more specifically to creeds, especially in religion. In the narrow sense the term means 'conforming to the Christian faith as represented in the creeds of the early Church'.

Polemic	A polemic is a contentious argument that is intended to establish the truth of a specific belief and the falsity of the contrary belief. Polemics are mostly seen in arguments about very controversial topics. The art or practice of such argumentation is called polemics.
Aristotle	Aristotle was a Greek philosopher and polymath, a student of Plato and teacher of Alexander the Great. His writings cover many subjects, including physics, metaphysics, poetry, theater, music, logic, rhetoric, linguistics, politics, government, ethics, biology, and zoology. Together with Plato and Socrates (Plato's teacher), Aristotle is one of the most important founding figures in Western philosophy.
Hippo	Hippo was a Presocratic Greek philosopher. He is variously described as coming from Rhegium, Metapontum, Samos, and Croton, and it is possible that there was more than one philosopher with this name. Although he was a natural philosopher, Aristotle refused to place him among the other great Pre-Socratic philosophers 'because of the paltriness of his thought.' At some point Hippo was accused of atheism, but as his works have perished, we cannot be certain why.
Metaphysics	Metaphysics is a branch of philosophy concerned with explaining the fundamental nature of being and the world, although the term is not easily defined. Traditionally, metaphysics attempts to answer two basic questions in the broadest possible terms:•'What is there?'•'What is it like?' A person who studies metaphysics is called a metaphysicist or a metaphysician. The metaphysician attempts to clarify the fundamental notions by which people understand the world, e.g., existence, objects and their properties, space and time, cause and effect, and possibility.
Quran	The Quran, also transliterated Qur'an, Koran, Al-Coran, Coran, Kuran, and Al-Qur'an, is the central religious text of Islam, which Muslims consider the verbatim word of God . It is regarded widely as the finest piece of literature in the Arabic language. The Quran is composed of verses (Ayah) that make up 114 chapters (suras) of unequal length which are classified either as Meccan or Medinan depending upon the place and time of their claimed revelation.
Demon	A demon is a supernatural, often malevolent being prevalent in religion, occultism, literature, and folklore. The original Greek word daimon does not carry the negative connotation initially understood by implementation of the Koine δαιμ?νιον (daimonion), and later ascribed to any cognate words sharing the root.

1. Comparative Practices in Global History: If Horses Had Hands

Albert Schweitzer	Albert Schweitzer OM (14 January 1875 - 4 September 1965) was a German and then French theologian, organist, philosopher, physician, and medical missionary. He was born in Kaysersberg in the province of Alsace-Lorraine, at that time part of the German Empire. Schweitzer, a Lutheran, challenged both the secular view of Jesus as depicted by historical-critical methodology current at his time in certain academic circles, as well as the traditional Christian view.
Salvation	Salvation, in religion, is the saving of the soul from sin and its consequences. It may also be called 'deliverance' or 'redemption' from sin and its effects. Depending on the religious tradition, salvation is considered to be caused either by the free will and grace of a deity (in theistic religions) or by personal responsibility and self-effort (e.g. in the sramanic and yogic traditions of India).
Neoplatonism	Neoplatonism is the modern term for a school of mystical philosophy that took shape in the 3rd century AD, based on the teachings of Plato and earlier Platonists, with its earliest contributor believed to be Plotinus, and his teacher Ammonius Saccas. Neoplatonism focused on the spiritual and cosmological aspects of Platonic thought, synthesizing Platonism with Egyptian and Jewish theology. However, Neoplatonists would have considered themselves simply Platonists, and the modern distinction is due to the perception that their philosophy contained sufficiently unique interpretations of Plato to make it substantially different from what Plato wrote and believed.
Criticism	Criticism is the practice of judging the merits and faults of something or someone in an intelligible (or articulate) way. •The judger is called 'the critic'.•To engage in criticism is 'to criticize'.•One specific item of criticism is called 'a criticism'. Criticism can be:•directed toward a person or an animal; at a group, authority or organization; at a specific behaviour; or at an object of some kind (an idea, a relationship, a condition, a process, or a thing).•personal (delivered directly from one person to another, in a personal capacity), or impersonal (expressing the view of an organization, and not aimed at anyone personally).•highly specific and detailed, or very abstract and general.•verbal (expressed in language) or non-verbal (expressed symbolically, or expressed through an action or a way of behaving).•explicit (the criticism is clearly stated) or implicit (a criticism is implied by what is being said, but it is not stated openly).•the result of critical thinking or spontaneous impulse. To criticize does not necessarily imply 'to find fault', but the word is often taken to mean the simple expression of an objection against prejudice, or a disapproval. Often criticism involves active disagreement, but it may only mean 'taking sides'.
Historical criticism	Historical criticism, is a branch of literary criticism that investigates the origins of ancient text in order to understand 'the world behind the text'.

	The primary goal of historical criticism is to ascertain the text's primitive or original meaning in its original historical context and its literal sense or sensus literalis historicus. The secondary goal seeks to establish a reconstruction of the historical situation of the author and recipients of the text.
Logos	Logos is an important term in philosophy, psychology, rhetoric, and religion. Originally a word meaning 'a ground', 'a plea', 'an opinion', 'an expectation', 'word,' 'speech,' 'account,' 'reason,' it became a technical term in philosophy, beginning with Heraclitus (ca. 535-475 BC), who used the term for a principle of order and knowledge. Ancient philosophers used the term in different ways.
Metaphor	A metaphor is a literary figure of speech that describes a subject by asserting that it is, on some point of comparison, the same as another otherwise unrelated object. Metaphor is a type of analogy and is closely related to other rhetorical figures of speech that achieve their effects via association, comparison or resemblance including allegory, hyperbole, and simile. One of the most prominent examples of a metaphor in English literature is the All the world's a stage monologue from As You Like It:All the world's a stage,And all the men and women merely players;They have their exits and their entrances; -- William Shakespeare, As You Like It, 2/7 This quote is a metaphor because the world is not literally a stage.
Magi	Magi is a term, used since at least the 4th century BCE, to denote a follower of Zoroaster, or rather, a follower of what the Hellenistic world associated Zoroaster with, which was - in the main - the ability to read the stars, and manipulate the fate that the stars foretold. The meaning prior to Hellenistic period is uncertain. Pervasive throughout the Eastern Mediterranean and Western Asia until late antiquity and beyond, Greek mágos 'Magian'/Magician was influenced by Greek goÄ"s, the older word for a practitioner of Magic, to include astrology, alchemy and other forms of esoteric knowledge.
Revelation	In religion and theology, revelation is the revealing or disclosing, through active or passive communication with a divine entity or entities. In general usage, the term is used to refer to the process by which God reveals knowledge of himself, his will, and his divine providence, to the world of human beings. In secondary usage, it refers to the resulting human knowledge about God, prophecy, and other divine things.
Manichaeism	Manichaeism was a major gnostic religion, originating in Sassanid era Babylonia. Although most of the original writings of the founding prophet Mani (c. 216-276 CE) have been lost, numerous translations and fragmentary texts have survived.

1. Comparative Practices in Global History: If Horses Had Hands

Dualism	In philosophy of mind, dualism is the assumption that mental phenomena are, in some respects, non-physical, or that the mind and body are not identical. Thus, it encompasses a set of views about the relationship between mind and matter, and is contrasted with other positions, such as physicalism, in the mind-body problem.
	Aristotle shared Plato's view of multiple souls, and further elaborated a hierarchical arrangement, corresponding to the distinctive functions of plants, animals and people: a nutritive soul of growth and metabolism, that all three share, a perceptive soul of pain, pleasure and desire, that only animals and people share, and the faculty of reason, that is unique to people only.
Sharia	Sharia law is the moral code and religious law of Islam. Sharia deals with many topics addressed by secular law, including crime, politics and economics, as well as personal matters such as sexual intercourse, hygiene, diet, prayer, and fasting. Though interpretations of sharia vary between cultures, in its strictest definition it is considered the infallible law of God--as opposed to the human interpretation of the laws (fiqh).
Attitude	Attitude as a term of fine art refers to the posture or gesture given to a figure by a painter or sculptor. It applies to the body and not to a mental state, but the arrangement of the body is presumed to serve a communicative or expressive purpose. An example of a conventional attitude in art is proskynesis to indicate respect toward God, emperors, clerics of high status, and religious icons; in Byzantine art, it is particularly characteristic in depictions of the emperor paying homage to Christ.
Violence	Violence is defined by the World Health Organization as the intentional use of physical force or power, threatened or actual, against oneself, another person, or against a group or community, that either results in or has a high likelihood of resulting in injury, death, psychological harm, maldevelopment or deprivation. This definition associates intentionality with the committing of the act itself, irrespective of the outcome it produces.
	Globally, violence takes the lives of more than 1.5 million people annually: just over 50% due to suicide, some 35% due to homicide, and just over 12% as a direct result of war or some other form of conflict.
I Ching	The I Ching or 'Yì Jing' (pinyin), also known as the Classic of Changes, Book of Changes and Zhouyi, is one of the oldest of the Chinese classic texts. The book contains a divination system comparable to Western geomancy or the West African Ifá system; in Western cultures and modern East Asia, it is still widely used for this purpose.
	Traditionally, the I Ching and its hexagrams were thought to pre-date recorded history, and based on traditional Chinese accounts, its origins trace back to the 3rd to the 2nd millennium BC.

Iconoclasm	Iconoclasm is the deliberate destruction of religious icons and other symbols or monuments, usually with religious or political motives. It is a frequent component of major political or religious changes. The term encompasses the more specific destruction of images of a ruler after his death or overthrow (damnatio memoriae), for example, following Akhenaten's death in Ancient Egypt.
Sufi	The lexical root of Sufi is variously traced to ØµÙÙ^Ù á¹£Å«f 'wool', referring either to the simple cloaks the early Muslim ascetics wore, or possibly to ØµÙŽÙØ§ á¹£afÄ 'purity'. The two were combined by al-Rudhabari who said, 'The Sufi is the one who wears wool on top of purity.' The wool cloaks were sometimes a designation of their initiation into the Sufi order. The early Sufi orders considered the wearing of this coat an imitation of Isa bin Maryam (Jesus).
Advaita Vedanta	Advaita Vedanta is considered to be the most influential and most dominant sub-school of the Vedanta school of Hindu philosophy. Other major sub-schools of Vedanta are Visish?advaita and Dvaita; while the minor ones include Suddhadvaita, Dvaitadvaita and Achintya Bhedabheda. Advaita (literally, non-duality) is a system of thought where 'Advaita' refers to the identity of the Self (Atman) and the Whole (Brahman).
Upanishads	The Upanishads are a collection of philosophical texts which form the theoretical basis for the Hindu religion. They are also known as Vedanta, the end of the Veda. In the purest sense, they are not Sruti (revealed truths) but rather commentaries which explain the essence of the veda (revealed knowledge).
Caste	A caste is a combined social system of occupation, endogamy, culture, social class, and political power. caste should not be confused with class, in that members of a caste are deemed to be alike in function or culture, whereas not all members of a defined class may be so alike. Although Indian society is often now associated with the word 'caste', it was first used by the Portuguese to describe inherited class status in their own European society.
Colonialism	Colonialism is the building and maintaining of colonies in one territory by people based elsewhere. Colonialism is a process whereby sovereignty over the colony is claimed by the metropole, who impose a new government and perhaps a new social structure and economy. Colonialism comprises unequal relationships between metropole and colony and between colonists and the indigenous population.
Purity	Purity (suddha) is an important concept within much of Theravada and Mahayana Buddhism, although the implications of the resultant moral purification may be viewed differently in the varying traditions. The aim is to purify the personality of the Buddhist practitioner so that all moral and character defilements and defects (kleshas such as anger, ignorance and lust) are wiped away and Nirvana can be obtained.

1. Comparative Practices in Global History: If Horses Had Hands

Theory	In mathematical logic, a theory (also called a formal theory) is a set of sentences in a formal language. Usually a deductive system is understood from context. An element $\phi \in T$ of a theory T is then called an axiom of the theory, and any sentence that follows from the axioms ($T \vdash \phi$) is called a theorem of the theory.
Dalit	Dalit, is a self-designation for a group of people traditionally regarded as of Untouchables and unsuitable for making personal relationships. Dalits are a mixed population of numerous caste groups all over South Asia, and speak various languages. While the caste system has been abolished under the Indian constitution, there is still discrimination and prejudice against Dalits in South Asia.
KabÄ«r	KabÄ«r (Hindi: à¤•à¤¬à¥€à¤°, Punjabi: à¨•à¨¬à©€à¨°, Urdu: Ú©Ø¨ÙŠØ±â€Ž (1440--1518) was a mystic composer and saint of India, whose literature has greatly influenced the Bhakti movement of India. The story is told that on one particular day of the year, anyone can become a disciple by having a master speak the name of God over him. It is common for those who live near the Ganges to take their morning bath there in the sacred waters.
Purana	The Puranas are a group of important Hindu religious texts, notably consisting of narratives of the history of the universe from creation to destruction, genealogies of kings, heroes, sages, and demigods, and descriptions of Hindu cosmology, philosophy, and geography. Puranas usually give prominence to a particular deity, employing an abundance of religious and philosophical concepts. They are usually written in the form of stories related by one person to another.
Sikhism	Sikhism is a panentheistic religion founded during the 15th century in the Punjab region, by Guru Nanak Dev and continued to progress with ten successive Sikh gurus (the last teaching being the holy scripture Guru Granth Sahib Ji). It is the fifth-largest organized religion in the world, with over 30 million Sikhs and one of the most steadily growing. This system of religious philosophy and expression has been traditionally known as the Gurmat (literally 'wisdom of the Guru').
Buddha	Usually Buddha refers to SiddhÄrtha Gautama , the historical founder of Buddhism, for this Buddha age, who adopted that title. He is sometimes referred to as Sakyamuni or The Buddha Gautama , in order to distinguish him from other Buddha s (cf. Buddha hood, enlightenment, nirvana.)
Buddhism	Buddhism is a religion and philosophy indigenous to the Indian subcontinent that encompasses a variety of traditions, beliefs, and practices largely based on teachings attributed to Siddhartha Gautama, who is commonly known as the Buddha . The Buddha lived and taught in the eastern part of Indian subcontinent some time between the 6th and 4th centuries BCE.

	He is recognized by Buddhists as an awakened or enlightened teacher who shared his insights to help sentient beings end suffering (dukkha) through eliminating ignorance (avidya), craving , and hatred, by way of understanding and seeing dependent origination (pratityasamutpada) and non-self (anatman), and thus attain the highest happiness, nirvana (nirvana). Two major branches of Buddhism are recognized: Theravada ('The School of the Elders') and Mahayana ('The Great Vehicle').
Confucianism	Confucianism is a Chinese ethical and philosophical system developed from the teachings of the Chinese philosopher Confucius . Confucianism originated as an 'ethical-sociopolitical teaching' during the Spring and Autumn Period, but later developed metaphysical and cosmological elements in the Han Dynasty. Following the abandonment of Legalism in China after the Qin Dynasty, Confucianism became the official state ideology of China, until it was replaced by the 'Three Principles of the People' ideology with the establishment of the Republic of China, and then Maoist Communism after the ROC was replaced by the People's Republic of China in Mainland China.
Confucius	Confucius was a Chinese teacher, editor, politician, and philosopher of the Spring and Autumn Period of Chinese history. The philosophy of Confucius emphasized personal and governmental morality, correctness of social relationships, justice and sincerity. His followers competed successfully with many other schools during the Hundred Schools of Thought era only to be suppressed in favor of the Legalists during the Qin Dynasty.
Daoism	In English, the words Daoism and Taoism are the subject of an ongoing controversy over the preferred romanization for naming this native Chinese philosophy and Chinese religion. The root Chinese word é" 'way, path' is romanized tao in the older Wade-Giles system and dào in the modern Pinyin system. The sometimes heated arguments over Taoism vs. Daoism involve sinology, phonemes, loanwords, and politics - not to mention whether Taoism should be pronounced or .

1. Comparative Practices in Global History: If Horses Had Hands

1. A _____ is one who is regarded as having great knowledge, wisdom and authority in a certain area, and who uses it to guide others . As a principle for the development of consciousness it leads the creation from unreality to reality, from the darkness of ignorance to the light of knowledge. In its purest form this principle manifests on earth as a divine incarnation (saint), a person with supreme knowledge about God and all creation.

   a. Bagar
   b. Punishment
   c. Racialism
   d. Guru

2. Sri _____ (December 30, 1879 - April 14, 1950), born Venkataraman Iyer, was a Hindu spiritual master ('jnani'). He was born to a Tamil-speaking Brahmin family in Tiruchuzhi, Tamil Nadu. After experiencing at age 16 what he later described as liberation (moksha), he left home for Arunachala, a mountain considered sacred by Hindus.

   a. Akka Mahadevi
   b. Maitreyi
   c. Ramana Maharshi
   d. Manavala Mamunigal

3. _____ FRS (12 February 1809 - 19 April 1882) was an English naturalist who established that all species of life have descended over time from common ancestors, and proposed the scientific theory that this branching pattern of evolution resulted from a process that he called natural selection. He published his theory with compelling evidence for evolution in his 1859 book On the Origin of Species. The scientific community and much of the general public came to accept evolution as a fact in his lifetime, but it was not until the emergence of the modern evolutionary synthesis from the 1930s to the 1950s that a broad consensus developed that natural selection was the basic mechanism of evolution.

   a. Henryk Batuta hoax
   b. Charles Robert Darwin
   c. Makkhali Gosala
   d. Manavala Mamunigal

4. File:Religious syms.svg _____ is the academic field of multi-disciplinary, secular study of religious beliefs, behaviors, and institutions. It describes, compares, interprets, and explains religion, emphasising systematic, historically-based, and cross-cultural perspectives.

   While theology attempts to understand the intentions of a supernatural force (such as deities), _____ tries to study human religious behavior and belief from outside any particular religious viewpoint.

   a. affirmation
   b. Maitreyi
   c. Makkhali Gosala
   d. Religious studies

5. _____ is the systematic mistreatment of an individual or group by another group. The most common forms are religious _____, ethnic _____, and political _____, though there is naturally some overlap between these terms. The inflicting of suffering, harassment, isolation, imprisonment, fear, or pain are all factors that may establish _____.

   a. Playing God
   b. Persecution
   c. Racialism
   d. Racism

1. d

2. c

3. b

4. d

5. b

You can take the complete Chapter Practice Test

for 1. Comparative Practices in Global History: If Horses Had Hands
on all key terms, persons, places, and concepts.

Online 99 Cents

http://www.JustTheFacts101.com

Use www.JustTheFacts101.com for all your study needs

including Facts101's online interactive problem solving labs in

chemistry, statistics, mathematics, and more.

2. Western Origins and History of the Modern Practice: From the Bible to ...

23

CHAPTER OUTLINE: KEY TERMS, PEOPLE, PLACES, CONCEPTS

	Marsilio Ficino
	Hermes Trismegistus
	Italian Renaissance
	Renaissance
	Humanism
	Ernst Bergmann
	Scholasticism
	Giordano Bruno
	Protestantism
	Society
	Authority
	Charisma
	Persecution
	Sola scriptura
	Quran
	Enlightenment
	Criticism
	Historical criticism
	Declaration
	Romanticism
	Deism

2. Western Origins and History of the Modern Practice: From the Bible to ...

CHAPTER OUTLINE: KEY TERMS, PEOPLE, PLACES, CONCEPTS

	Natural theology
	All Religions are One
	William Blake
	Divinity
	Humanities
	Thomas Hobbes
	Consciousness
	Critical theory
	Idealism
	John Calvin
	Friedrich
	Gospel
	Richard Simon
	Spinoza
	Mysticism
	Philosophical analysis
	Myth and ritual
	Ernest Renan
	Religious studies
	Adam and Eve
	Advaita Vedanta

2. Western Origins and History of the Modern Practice: From the Bible to ...

25

CHAPTER OUTLINE: KEY TERMS, PEOPLE, PLACES, CONCEPTS

	Charles Robert Darwin
	Darwinism
	Upanishads
	Colonialism
	CoSMoS
	Creation myth
	Panentheism
	Religious experience
	East India Company
	Metaphor
	Modernity
	Orientalism
	Ralph Waldo Emerson
	Spiritual But Not Religious
	Transcendentalism
	Representation
	Spiritualism
	Spirituality
	Theosophy
	Annie Besant
	Buddhism

Materialism

Paranormal

Salvation

Marxism

Psychology

Cicero

Civil Rights

Feminist theology

Justice

Patriarchy

Social justice

Theology

Transcendence

Swami Niranjanananda

Swami Vivekananda

Daoism

Caste

Tantra

Yoga

Perennial philosophy

Rumi

2. Western Origins and History of the Modern Practice: From the Bible to ...

27

CHAPTER OUTLINE: KEY TERMS, PEOPLE, PLACES, CONCEPTS

	Huston Cummings Smith
	Sufi
	Constructivism
	Kwame Anthony Appiah
	Contextualism
	Cosmogony
	Cosmopolitanism
	Skepticism

CHAPTER HIGHLIGHTS & NOTES: KEY TERMS, PEOPLE, PLACES, CONCEPTS

Marsilio Ficino	Marsilio Ficino was one of the most influential humanist philosophers of the early Italian Renaissance, an astrologer, a reviver of Neoplatonism who was in touch with every major academic thinker and writer of his day, and the first translator of Plato's complete extant works into Latin. His Florentine Academy, an attempt to revive Plato's school, had enormous influence on the direction and tenor of the Italian Renaissance and the development of European philosophy. Ficino was born at Figline Valdarno.
Hermes Trismegistus	MythologyHermes Trismegistus Â· Thoth Â· Poimandres HermeticaCorpus Hermeticum Â· Kybalion Three Parts of the Wisdom of the Whole UniverseAlchemy Â· Astrology Â· Theurgy Influence and Influences Hermetic MovementsRosicrucianism

2. Western Origins and History of the Modern Practice: From the Bible to ...

CHAPTER HIGHLIGHTS & NOTES: KEY TERMS, PEOPLE, PLACES, CONCEPTS

	OrdersHermetic Order of the Golden Dawn Â· Hermetic Brotherhood of Luxor Â· Hermetic Brotherhood of Light Topics in HermetismQabalah Occult and divinatory tarot Hermetists and HermeticistsJohn Dee . Aleister Crowley Â· Israel RegardieThÄbit ibn Qurra Â· ParacelsusGiordano Bruno Â· Manly P. Hall Â· Samuel MacGregor Mathers Â· William WestcottFranz BardonHermes Trismegistus is the representation of the combination of the Greek god Hermes and the Egyptian god Thoth. In Hellenistic Egypt, the Greeks recognised the congruence of their God Hermes with the Egyptian god Thoth.
Italian Renaissance	The Italian Renaissance was the earliest manifestation of the general European Renaissance, a period of great cultural change and achievement that began in Italy around the end of the 13th century and lasted until the 16th century, marking the transition between Medieval and Early Modern Europe. The term Renaissance is in essence a modern one that came into currency in the 19th century, in the work of historians such as Jacob Burckhardt. Although the origins of a movement that was confined largely to the literate culture of intellectual endeavor and patronage can be traced to the earlier part of the 14th century, many aspects of Italian culture and society remained largely Medieval; the Renaissance did not come into full swing until the end of the century.
Renaissance	The Renaissance was a cultural movement that spanned the period roughly from the 14th to the 17th century, beginning in Italy in the Late Middle Ages and later spreading to the rest of Europe. Though the invention of printing sped the dissemination of ideas from the later 15th century, the changes of the Renaissance were not uniformly experienced across Europe. As a cultural movement, it encompassed innovative flowering of Latin and vernacular literatures, beginning with the 14th-century resurgence of learning based on classical sources, which contemporaries credited to Petrarch, the development of linear perspective and other techniques of rendering a more natural reality in painting, and gradual but widespread educational reform.
Humanism	Humanism is an approach in study, philosophy, world view, or practice that focuses on human values and concerns, attaching prime importance to human rather than divine or supernatural matters. According to Greg M. Epstein, 'Humanism today can be categorized as a movement, a philosophy of life or worldview, or ... [a] lifestance.' In philosophy and social science, humanism is a perspective which affirms some notion of human nature, and is contrasted with anti-humanism. Secular humanism is a secular ideology that espouses reason, ethics, and justice, whilst specifically rejecting supernatural and religious dogma as a basis of morality and decision-making.
Ernst Bergmann	Ernst Bergmann (7 August 1881, Colditz, Kingdom of Saxony - 16 April 1945, Naumburg) was a German philosopher and proponent of Nazism.

2. Western Origins and History of the Modern Practice: From the Bible to ...

29

CHAPTER HIGHLIGHTS & NOTES: KEY TERMS, PEOPLE, PLACES, CONCEPTS

	He studied philosophy and German philology at the University of Leipzig and got his PhD in 1905. Subsequently he continued his studies in Berlin. Later he returned to Leipzig, where he received the status of Privatdozent at the university in 1911. In 1916 he was awarded the position of Ausserordentlicher Professor (professor without chair).
Scholasticism	Scholasticism is a method of critical thought which dominated teaching by the academics (scholastics, or schoolmen) of medieval universities in Europe from about 1100-1500, and a program of employing that method in articulating and defending orthodoxy in an increasingly pluralistic context. It originated as an outgrowth of, and a departure from, Christian monastic schools. Not so much a philosophy or a theology as a method of learning, scholasticism places a strong emphasis on dialectical reasoning to extend knowledge by inference, and to resolve contradictions.
Giordano Bruno	Giordano Bruno born Filippo Bruno, was an Italian Dominican friar, philosopher, mathematician and astronomer. His cosmological theories went beyond the Copernican model in proposing that the Sun was essentially a star, and moreover, that the universe contained an infinite number of inhabited worlds populated by other intelligent beings. He was burned at the stake by civil authorities in 1600 after the Roman Inquisition found him guilty of heresy for his pantheism and turned him over to the state, which at that time considered heresy illegal.
Protestantism	Protestantism is a branch within Christianity, containing many denominations of different practices and doctrines, that originated in the sixteenth-century Protestant Reformation. It is considered to be one of the primary divisions within the original Christian church, i.e., the Catholic Church, along with Eastern Orthodoxy. Some groups that are often loosely labeled 'Protestant' do not use the term to define themselves, and some tend to reject it because of the implication of being non-traditional.
Society	A society, or a human society, is a group of people involved with each other through persistent relations, or a large social grouping sharing the same geographical or social territory, subject to the same political authority and dominant cultural expectations. Human societies are characterized by patterns of relationships (social relations) between individuals who share a distinctive culture and institutions; a given society may be described as the sum total of such relationships among its constituent members. In the social sciences, a larger society often evinces stratification and/or dominance patterns in subgroups.
Authority	Authority is the legitimate or socially approved use of power. It is the legitimate power which one person or a group holds over another. The element of legitimacy is vital to the notion of authority and is the main means by which authority is distinguished from the more general concept of power.

2. Western Origins and History of the Modern Practice: From the Bible to ...

Charisma	The term charisma has two senses: 1) compelling attractiveness or charm that can inspire devotion in others, 2) a divinely conferred power or talent. For some theological usages the term is rendered charism, with a meaning the same as sense 2.
Persecution	Persecution is the systematic mistreatment of an individual or group by another group. The most common forms are religious persecution, ethnic persecution, and political persecution, though there is naturally some overlap between these terms. The inflicting of suffering, harassment, isolation, imprisonment, fear, or pain are all factors that may establish persecution.
Sola scriptura	Sola scriptura is the doctrine that the Bible is the only infallible or inerrant authority for Christian faith, and that it contains all knowledge necessary for salvation and holiness. Consequently, Sola scriptura demands that no doctrine is to be admitted or confessed that is not found directly or logically within Scripture. However, Sola scriptura is not a denial of other authorities governing Christian life and devotion.
Quran	The Quran, also transliterated Qur'an, Koran, Al-Coran, Coran, Kuran, and Al-Qur'an, is the central religious text of Islam, which Muslims consider the verbatim word of God . It is regarded widely as the finest piece of literature in the Arabic language. The Quran is composed of verses (Ayah) that make up 114 chapters (suras) of unequal length which are classified either as Meccan or Medinan depending upon the place and time of their claimed revelation.
Enlightenment	Enlightenment in a secular context often means the 'full comprehension of a situation', but in spiritual terms the word alludes to a spiritual revelation or deep insight into the meaning and purpose of all things, communication with or understanding of the mind of God, profound spiritual understanding or a fundamentally changed consciousness whereby everything is perceived as a unity. Some scientists believe that during meditative states leading up to the subjective experience of enlightenment there are actual physical changes in the brain. Buddhism The English term 'enlightenment' has commonly been used to translate several Sanskrit, Pali, Chinese and Japanese terms and concepts, especially bodhi, prajna, kensho, satori and buddhahood.
Criticism	Criticism is the practice of judging the merits and faults of something or someone in an intelligible (or articulate) way. •The judger is called 'the critic'.•To engage in criticism is 'to criticize'.•One specific item of criticism is called 'a criticism'.

2. Western Origins and History of the Modern Practice: From the Bible to ...

31

CHAPTER HIGHLIGHTS & NOTES: KEY TERMS, PEOPLE, PLACES, CONCEPTS

Criticism can be:•directed toward a person or an animal; at a group, authority or organization; at a specific behaviour; or at an object of some kind (an idea, a relationship, a condition, a process, or a thing).•personal (delivered directly from one person to another, in a personal capacity), or impersonal (expressing the view of an organization, and not aimed at anyone personally).•highly specific and detailed, or very abstract and general.•verbal (expressed in language) or non-verbal (expressed symbolically, or expressed through an action or a way of behaving).•explicit (the criticism is clearly stated) or implicit (a criticism is implied by what is being said, but it is not stated openly).•the result of critical thinking or spontaneous impulse.

To criticize does not necessarily imply 'to find fault', but the word is often taken to mean the simple expression of an objection against prejudice, or a disapproval. Often criticism involves active disagreement, but it may only mean 'taking sides'.

Historical criticism	
	Historical criticism, is a branch of literary criticism that investigates the origins of ancient text in order to understand 'the world behind the text'.

The primary goal of historical criticism is to ascertain the text's primitive or original meaning in its original historical context and its literal sense or sensus literalis historicus. The secondary goal seeks to establish a reconstruction of the historical situation of the author and recipients of the text. |
Declaration	In law, a declaration is a binding adjudication of the rights or other legal relations of the parties which does not provide for or order enforcement. Where the declaration is made by a court, it is usually referred to as a declaratory judgment. Less commonly, where declaratory relief is awarded by an arbitrator, it is normally called a declaratory award.
Romanticism	Romanticism was an artistic, literary, and intellectual movement that originated in Europe toward the end of the 18th century and in most areas was at its peak in the approximate period from 1800 to 1840. Partly a reaction to the Industrial Revolution, it was also a revolt against aristocratic social and political norms of the Age of Enlightenment and a reaction against the scientific rationalization of nature. It was embodied most strongly in the visual arts, music, and literature, but had a major impact on historiography, education and the natural sciences. Its effect on politics was considerable, and complex; while for much of the peak Romantic period it was associated with liberalism and radicalism, in the long term its effect on the growth of nationalism was probably more significant.
Deism	Deism is a religious philosophy which holds that reason and observation of the natural world, without the need for organized religion, can determine that the universe is the product of an intelligent creator. According to deists, the creator never intervenes in human affairs or suspends the natural laws of the universe.

2. Western Origins and History of the Modern Practice: From the Bible to ...

Natural theology	Natural theology is a branch of theology based on reason and ordinary experience. Thus it is distinguished from revealed theology which is based on scripture and religious experiences of various kinds; and also from transcendental theology, theology from a priori reasoning. Marcus Terentius Varro (116-27 BC) in his (lost) Antiquitates rerum humanarum et divinarum established a distinction of three kinds of theology: civil (political) (theologia civilis), natural (physical) (theologia naturalis) and mythical (theologia mythica).
All Religions are One	All Religions are One is the title of a series of philosophical aphorisms by William Blake, written in 1788. Following on from his initial experiments with relief etching in the non-textual The Approach of Doom (1787), All Religions are One and There is No Natural Religion represent Blake's first successful attempt to combine image and text via relief etching, and are thus the earliest of his illuminated manuscripts. As such, they serve as a significant milestone in Blake's career; as Peter Ackroyd points out, 'his newly invented form now changed the nature of his expression. It had enlarged his range; with relief etching, the words inscribed like those of God upon the tables of law, Blake could acquire a new role.' In 1822, Blake completed a short two-page dramatic piece which would prove to be the last of his illuminated manuscripts, entitled The Ghost of Abel A Revelation In the Visions of Jehovah Seen by William Blake.
William Blake	William Blake (28 November 1757 - 12 August 1827) was an English poet, painter, and printmaker. Largely unrecognised during his lifetime, Blake is now considered a seminal figure in the history of both the poetry and visual arts of the Romantic Age. His prophetic poetry has been said to form 'what is in proportion to its merits the least read body of poetry in the English language'.
Divinity	Divinity is the study of Christian and other theology and ministry at a school, divinity school, university, or seminary. The term is sometimes a synonym for theology as an academic, speculative pursuit, and sometimes is used for the study of applied theology and ministry to make a distinction between that and academic theology. It most often refers to Christian study which is linked with the professional degrees for ordained ministry or related work, though it is also used in an academic setting by other faith traditions.
Humanities	The humanities are academic disciplines that study the human condition, using methods that are primarily analytical, critical, or speculative, as distinguished from the mainly empirical approaches of the natural sciences. The humanities include ancient and modern languages, literature, history, philosophy, religion, and visual and performing arts such as music and theatre. The humanities that are also regarded as social sciences include technology, history, anthropology, area studies, communication studies, cultural studies, law and linguistics.

2. Western Origins and History of the Modern Practice: From the Bible to ...

33

Thomas Hobbes	Thomas Hobbes of Malmesbury (5 April 1588 - 4 December 1679), in some older texts Thomas Hobbs of Malmsbury, was an English philosopher, best known today for his work on political philosophy. His 1651 book Leviathan established the foundation for most of Western political philosophy from the perspective of social contract theory. Hobbes was a champion of absolutism for the sovereign but he also developed some of the fundamentals of European liberal thought: the right of the individual; the natural equality of all men; the artificial character of the political order (which led to the later distinction between civil society and the state); the view that all legitimate political power must be 'representative' and based on the consent of the people; and a liberal interpretation of law which leaves people free to do whatever the law does not explicitly forbid.
Consciousness	Consciousness is the quality or state of being aware of an external object or something within oneself. It has been defined as: subjectivity, awareness, the ability to experience or to feel, wakefulness, having a sense of selfhood, and the executive control system of the mind. Despite the difficulty in definition, many philosophers believe that there is a broadly shared underlying intuition about what consciousness is.
Critical theory	Critical theory is a school of thought that stresses the examination and critique of society and culture, drawing from knowledge across the social sciences and humanities. The term has two different meanings with different origins and histories: one originating in sociology and the other in literary criticism. This has led to the very literal use of 'critical theory' as an umbrella term to describe any theory founded upon critique.
Idealism	In philosophy, idealism is the group of philosophies which assert that reality, or reality as we can know it, is fundamentally mental, mentally constructed, or otherwise immaterial. Epistemologically, idealism manifests as a skepticism about the possibility of knowing any mind-independent thing. In a sociological sense, idealism emphasizes how human ideas -- especially beliefs and values -- shape society.
John Calvin	John Calvin was an influential French theologian and pastor during the Protestant Reformation. He was a principal figure in the development of the system of Christian theology later called Calvinism. Originally trained as a humanist lawyer, he broke from the Roman Catholic Church around 1530. After religious tensions provoked a violent uprising against Protestants in France, Calvin fled to Basel, Switzerland, where in 1536 he published the first edition of his seminal work Institutes of the Christian Religion.
Friedrich	The Friedrich are the most ancient German-Bohemian glass-maker family. History

2. Western Origins and History of the Modern Practice: From the Bible to ...

	From as early as 750 years ago, the shadowy picture of the oldest German-Bohemian glass-maker family Friedrich emerges, who contributed greatly towards the creation of the world-famous Bohemian glass (also called Bohemian Crystal). In pre-Hussite times they produced amazing works of vitreous art near Daubitz, nowadays called Doubice.
Gospel	A Gospel is a writing that describes the life of Jesus. The word is primarily used to refer to the four canonical Gospels: the Gospel of Matthew, Gospel of Mark, Gospel of Luke and Gospel of John, probably written between AD 65 and 80. They appear to have been originally untitled; they were quoted anonymously in the first half of the second century (i.e. 100-150) but the names by which they are currently known appear suddenly around the year 180.
	The first canonical Gospel written is thought by most scholars to be Mark (c 65-70), which was according to the majority used as a source for the Gospels of Matthew and Luke.
Richard Simon	Richard Simon was a French biblical critic.
	He was born at Dieppe. His early education took place at the college of the Fathers of the Oratory.
Spinoza	Baruch or Benedict de Spinoza was a Dutch philosopher of Portuguese Jewish origin. Revealing considerable scientific aptitude, the breadth and importance of Spinoza's work was not fully realized until years after his death. Today, he is considered one of the great rationalists of 17th-century philosophy, laying the groundwork for the 18th century Enlightenment and modern biblical criticism.
Mysticism	Mysticism is the pursuit of communion with, identity with divinity, spiritual truth intuition, instinct or insight. Mysticism usually centers on a practice or practices intended to nurture those experiences or awareness. Mysticism may be dualistic, maintaining a distinction between the self and the divine, or may be nondualistic.
Philosophical analysis	Philosophical analysis is a general term for techniques typically used by philosophers in the analytic tradition that involve 'breaking down' (i.e. analyzing) philosophical issues.
Myth and ritual	In traditional societies, Myth and ritual are two central components of religious practice. Although Myth and ritual are commonly united as parts of religion, the exact relationship between them has been a matter of controversy among scholars. One of the approaches to this problem is 'the Myth and ritual, or myth-ritualist, theory', which holds that 'myth does not stand by itself but is tied to ritual'.
Ernest Renan	Joseph Ernest Renan was a French expert of Middle East ancient languages and civilizations, philosopher and writer, devoted to his native province of Brittany.

2. Western Origins and History of the Modern Practice: From the Bible to ...

35

CHAPTER HIGHLIGHTS & NOTES: KEY TERMS, PEOPLE, PLACES, CONCEPTS

	He is best known for his influential historical works on early Christianity and his political theories, especially concerning nationalism and national identity. Birth and family
	He was born at Tréguier in Brittany to a family of fishermen.
Religious studies	File:Religious syms.svg Religious studies is the academic field of multi-disciplinary, secular study of religious beliefs, behaviors, and institutions. It describes, compares, interprets, and explains religion, emphasising systematic, historically-based, and cross-cultural perspectives.
	While theology attempts to understand the intentions of a supernatural force (such as deities), religious studies tries to study human religious behavior and belief from outside any particular religious viewpoint.
Adam and Eve	Adam and Eve were, according to the Book of Genesis, the first man and woman created by YHWH . In theology and in folklore studies, the technical term 'protoplasts' is sometimes used for the first humans in this sense.
	Narrative
	Genesis 2
	Genesis 2 opens with God fashioning a man from the dust and blowing life into his nostrils.
Advaita Vedanta	Advaita Vedanta is considered to be the most influential and most dominant sub-school of the Vedanta school of Hindu philosophy. Other major sub-schools of Vedanta are Visish?advaita and Dvaita; while the minor ones include Suddhadvaita, Dvaitadvaita and Achintya Bhedabheda.
	Advaita (literally, non-duality) is a system of thought where 'Advaita' refers to the identity of the Self (Atman) and the Whole (Brahman).
Charles Robert Darwin	Charles Robert Darwin FRS (12 February 1809 - 19 April 1882) was an English naturalist who established that all species of life have descended over time from common ancestors, and proposed the scientific theory that this branching pattern of evolution resulted from a process that he called natural selection. He published his theory with compelling evidence for evolution in his 1859 book On the Origin of Species. The scientific community and much of the general public came to accept evolution as a fact in his lifetime, but it was not until the emergence of the modern evolutionary synthesis from the 1930s to the 1950s that a broad consensus developed that natural selection was the basic mechanism of evolution.
Darwinism	Darwinism is a set of movements and concepts related to ideas of transmutation of species or evolution, including ideas with no connection to the work of Charles Darwin. The meaning of 'Darwinism' has changed over time, and varies depending on who is using the term.

2. Western Origins and History of the Modern Practice: From the Bible to ...

Upanishads	The Upanishads are a collection of philosophical texts which form the theoretical basis for the Hindu religion. They are also known as Vedanta, the end of the Veda. In the purest sense, they are not Sruti (revealed truths) but rather commentaries which explain the essence of the veda (revealed knowledge).
Colonialism	Colonialism is the building and maintaining of colonies in one territory by people based elsewhere. Colonialism is a process whereby sovereignty over the colony is claimed by the metropole, who impose a new government and perhaps a new social structure and economy. Colonialism comprises unequal relationships between metropole and colony and between colonists and the indigenous population.
CoSMoS	CoSMoS is a UK funded research project seeking do build capacity in generic modelling tools and simulation techniques for complex systems. Its acronym stands for Complex Systems Modelling and Simulation. This is a four-year project, running from 2007 to 2011 as a collaboration between the University of York and Kent, with further collaborations from the University of Abertay Dundee and Bristol Robotics Laboratory.
Creation myth	A creation myth is a symbolic narrative of a culture, tradition or people that describes their earliest beginnings, how the world they know began and how they first came into it. Creation myths develop in oral traditions, and are the most common form of myth, found throughout human culture. In the society in which it is told, a creation myth is usually regarded as conveying profound truths, although not necessarily in a historical or literal sense.
Panentheism	Panentheism (from Greek π?v (pân) 'all'; ?v (en) 'in'; and θε?ς (theós) 'God'; 'all-in-God') is a belief system which posits that the divine exists (be it a monotheistic God, polytheistic gods, or an eternal cosmic animating force), interpenetrates every part of nature and timelessly extends beyond it. Panentheism differentiates itself from pantheism, which holds that the divine is synonymous with the universe. In panentheism, the universe in the first formulation is practically the whole itself.
Religious experience	A religious experience is a subjective experience in which an individual reports contact with a transcendent reality, an encounter or union with the divine. Such an experience often involves arriving at some knowledge or insight previously unavailable to the subject yet unnaccountable or unforseeable according to the usual conceptual or psychological framework within which the subject has been used to operating. Religious experience generally brings understanding, partial or complete, of issues of a fundamental character that may have been a cause (whether consciously ackowledged or not) of anguish or alienation to the subject for an extended period of time.
East India Company	The East India Company was an early English joint-stock company that was formed initially for pursuing trade with the East Indies, but that ended up trading mainly with the Indian subcontinent and China.

2. Western Origins and History of the Modern Practice: From the Bible to ...

37

CHAPTER HIGHLIGHTS & NOTES: KEY TERMS, PEOPLE, PLACES, CONCEPTS

	The oldest among several similarly formed European East India Companies, the Company was granted an English Royal Charter, under the name Governor and Company of Merchants of London Trading into the East Indies, by Elizabeth I on 31 December 1600. After a rival English company challenged its monopoly in the late 17th century, the two companies were merged in 1708 to form the United Company of Merchants of England Trading to the East Indies, commonly styled the Honourable East India Company, and abbreviated, HEIC; the Company was colloquially referred to as John Company, and in India as Company Bahadur .
	The East India Company traded mainly in cotton, silk, indigo dye, saltpetre, tea, and opium.
Metaphor	A metaphor is a literary figure of speech that describes a subject by asserting that it is, on some point of comparison, the same as another otherwise unrelated object. Metaphor is a type of analogy and is closely related to other rhetorical figures of speech that achieve their effects via association, comparison or resemblance including allegory, hyperbole, and simile.
	One of the most prominent examples of a metaphor in English literature is the All the world's a stage monologue from As You Like It:All the world's a stage,And all the men and women merely players;They have their exits and their entrances; -- William Shakespeare, As You Like It, 2/7
	This quote is a metaphor because the world is not literally a stage.
Modernity	Modernity typically refers to a post-traditional, post-medieval historical period, one marked by the move from feudalism (or agrarianism) toward capitalism, industrialization, secularization, rationalization, the nation-state and its constituent institutions and forms of surveillance (Barker 2005, 444). Conceptually, modernity relates to the modern era and to modernism, but forms a distinct concept. Whereas the Enlightenment invokes a specific movement in Western philosophy, modernity tends to refer only to the social relations associated with the rise of capitalism.
Orientalism	Orientalism is a term used by art historians, literary and cultural studies scholars for the imitation or depiction of aspects of Middle Eastern, and East Asian cultures (Eastern cultures) by American and European writers, designers and artists. In particular, Orientalist painting, depicting more specifically 'the Middle East', was one of the many specialisms of 19th century Academic art. Since the publication of Edward Said's Orientalism, the term has arguably acquired a negative connotation.
Ralph Waldo Emerson	Ralph Waldo Emerson was an American essayist, lecturer, and poet, who led the Transcendentalist movement of the mid-19th century. He was seen as a champion of individualism and a prescient critic of the countervailing pressures of society, and he disseminated his thoughts through dozens of published essays and more than 1,500 public lectures across the United States.

2. Western Origins and History of the Modern Practice: From the Bible to ...

Spiritual But Not Religious	Spiritual But Not Religious is a popular phrase and acronym used to self-identify a life stance of spirituality that rejects traditional organized religion as the sole or most valuable means of furthering spiritual growth. The term is used world-wide, but seems most prominent in the United States where one study reports that as many as 33% of people identify as spiritual but not religious. Other surveys report lower percentages ranging from 24%-10% Those that identify as SBNR vary in their individual spiritual philosophies and practices and theological references.
Transcendentalism	Transcendentalism was a group of new ideas in literature, religion, culture, and philosophy that emerged in New England in the early to middle 19th century. It is sometimes called American Transcendentalism to distinguish it from other uses of the word transcendental. Transcendentalism began as a protest against the general state of culture and society, and in particular, the state of intellectualism at Harvard and the doctrine of the Unitarian church taught at Harvard Divinity School.
Representation	Representation is the use of signs that stand in for and take the place of something else. It is through representation that people organize the world and reality through the act of naming its elements. Signs are arranged in order to form semantic constructions and express relations.
Spiritualism	Spiritualism is a dualist metaphysical belief that the world is made up of at least two fundamental substances, matter and spirit. This very broad metaphysical distinction is further developed into many and various forms by the inclusion of details about what spiritual entities exist such as a soul, the afterlife, spirits of the dead, deities and mediums; as well as details about the nature of the relationship between spirit and matter. It may also refer to the philosophy, doctrine, or religion pertaining to a spiritual aspect of existence.
Spirituality	Spirituality refers to an ultimate or an alleged immaterial reality; an inner path enabling a person to discover the essence of his/her being; or the 'deepest values and meanings by which people live.' Spiritual practices, including meditation, prayer and contemplation, are intended to develop an individual's inner life; spiritual experience includes that of connectedness with a larger reality, yielding a more comprehensive self; with other individuals or the human community; with nature or the cosmos; or with the divine realm. Spirituality is often experienced as a source of inspiration or orientation in life. It can encompass belief in immaterial realities or experiences of the immanent or transcendent nature of the world.
Theosophy	Theosophy, refers to systems of esoteric philosophy concerning, or investigation seeking direct knowledge of, presumed mysteries of being and nature, particularly concerning the nature of divinity.

2. Western Origins and History of the Modern Practice: From the Bible to ...

39

CHAPTER HIGHLIGHTS & NOTES: KEY TERMS, PEOPLE, PLACES, CONCEPTS

	Theosophy is considered a part of the broader field of esotericism, referring to hidden knowledge or wisdom that offers the individual enlightenment and salvation. The word esoteric dates back to the 2nd century CE. The theosophist seeks to understand the mysteries of the universe and the bonds that unite the universe, humanity and the divine.
Annie Besant	Annie Besant was a prominent Theosophist, women's rights activist, writer and orator and supporter of Irish and Indian self rule. She was married at 19 to Frank Besant but separated from him over religious differences. Moving to London, she became a prominent speaker for the National Secular Society and writer and a close friend of Charles Bradlaugh.
Buddhism	Buddhism is a religion and philosophy indigenous to the Indian subcontinent that encompasses a variety of traditions, beliefs, and practices largely based on teachings attributed to Siddhartha Gautama, who is commonly known as the Buddha . The Buddha lived and taught in the eastern part of Indian subcontinent some time between the 6th and 4th centuries BCE. He is recognized by Buddhists as an awakened or enlightened teacher who shared his insights to help sentient beings end suffering (dukkha) through eliminating ignorance (avidya), craving , and hatred, by way of understanding and seeing dependent origination (pratityasamutpada) and non-self (anatman), and thus attain the highest happiness, nirvana (nirvana). Two major branches of Buddhism are recognized: Theravada ('The School of the Elders') and Mahayana ('The Great Vehicle').
Materialism	In philosophy, the theory of materialism holds that the only thing that exists is matter or energy; that all things are composed of material and all phenomena (including consciousness) are the result of material interactions. In other words, matter is the only substance, and reality is identical with the actually occurring states of energy and matter. To many philosophers, 'materialism' is synonymous with 'physicalism'.
Paranormal	Paranormal is a general term that describes unusual experiences that supposedly lack a scientific explanation, or phenomena alleged to be outside of science's current ability to explain or measure. Notably, Paranormal phenomena also lack scientific evidence, as detectable but not well explained phenomena such as dark matter or dark energy are not commonly called Paranormal. In parapsychology, the term has, in the past, been used to describe the supposed phenomena of extra-sensory perception, including telepathy, and psychokinesis, ghosts, and hauntings.
Salvation	Salvation, in religion, is the saving of the soul from sin and its consequences. It may also be called 'deliverance' or 'redemption' from sin and its effects.

2. Western Origins and History of the Modern Practice: From the Bible to ...

CHAPTER HIGHLIGHTS & NOTES: KEY TERMS, PEOPLE, PLACES, CONCEPTS

	Depending on the religious tradition, salvation is considered to be caused either by the free will and grace of a deity (in theistic religions) or by personal responsibility and self-effort (e.g. in the sramanic and yogic traditions of India).
Marxism	Marxism is an economic and sociopolitical worldview and method of socioeconomic inquiry centered upon a materialist interpretation of history, a dialectical view of social change, and an analysis-critique of the development of capitalism. In the early-to-mid 19th century, the intellectual development of Marxism was pioneered by two German philosophers, Karl Marx and Friedrich Engels. As an ideology, Marxism encompasses an economic theory, a sociological theory, and a revolutionary view of social change.
Psychology	Psychology is an academic and applied discipline that involves the scientific study of mental functions and behaviors. Psychology has the immediate goal of understanding individuals and groups by both establishing general principles and researching specific cases, and by many accounts it ultimately aims to benefit society. In this field, a professional practitioner or researcher is called a psychologist and can be classified as a social, behavioral, or cognitive scientist.
Cicero	Marcus Tullius Cicero was a Roman philosopher, statesman, lawyer, orator, political theorist, Roman consul and constitutionalist. He came from a wealthy municipal family of the equestrian order, and is widely considered one of Rome's greatest orators and prose stylists. He introduced the Romans to the chief schools of Greek philosophy and created a Latin philosophical vocabulary (with neologisms such as humanitas, qualitas, quantitas, and essentia) distinguishing himself as a linguist, translator, and philosopher.
Civil Rights	Civil and political rights are a class of rights that protect individuals' freedom from unwarranted infringement by governments and private organizations, and ensure one's ability to participate in the civil and political life of the state without discrimination or repression. Civil rights include the ensuring of peoples' physical and mental integrity, life and safety; protection from discrimination on grounds such as race, gender, sexual orientation, gender identity, national origin, colour, ethnicity, religion, or disability; and individual rights such as privacy, the freedoms of thought and conscience, speech and expression, religion, the press, assembly and movement. Political rights include natural justice in law, such as the rights of the accused, including the right to a fair trial; due process; the right to seek redress or a legal remedy; and rights of participation in civil society and politics such as freedom of association, the right to assemble, the right to petition, the right of self-defense, and the right to vote.

2. Western Origins and History of the Modern Practice: From the Bible to ...

41

Feminist theology	Feminist theology is a movement found in several religions, including Buddhism, Christianity, Judaism, and New Thought, to reconsider the traditions, practices, scriptures, and theologies of those religions from a feminist perspective. Some of the goals of feminist theology include increasing the role of women among the clergy and religious authorities, reinterpreting male-dominated imagery and language about God, determining women's place in relation to career and motherhood, and studying images of women in the religion's sacred texts and matriarchal religion. Feminist theology attempts to consider every aspect of religious practice and thought.
Justice	Justice is a concept of moral rightness based on ethics, rationality, law, natural law, religion, or equity. It is also the act of being just and/or fair. According to most contemporary theories of justice, justice is overwhelmingly important: John Rawls claims that 'Justice is the first virtue of social institutions, as truth is of systems of thought.' Justice can be thought of as distinct from and more fundamental than benevolence, charity, mercy, generosity, or compassion.
Patriarchy	Patriarchy is a social system in which the role of the male as the primary authority figure is central to social organization, and where fathers hold authority over women, children, and property. It implies the institutions of male rule and privilege, and is dependent on female subordination. Historically, the principle of patriarchy has been central to the social, legal, political, and economic organization of Celtic, Germanic, Roman, Greek, Hebrew, Arabian, Indian, and Chinese cultures, and has had a deep influence on modern civilization.
Social justice	Social justice generally refers to the idea of creating a society or institution that is based on the principles of equality and solidarity, that understands and values human rights, and that recognizes the dignity of every human being. Social justice is based on the concepts of human rights and equality and involves a greater degree of economic egalitarianism through progressive taxation, income redistribution, or even property redistribution. These policies aim to achieve what developmental economists refer to as more equality of opportunity than may currently exist in some societies, and to manufacture equality of outcome in cases where incidental inequalities appear in a procedurally just system.
Theology	Theology is the rational and systematic study of religion and its influences and of the nature of religious truth, or the learned profession acquired by specialized courses in religion, usually taught at a college or seminary. Augustine of Hippo defined the Latin equivalent, theologia, as 'reasoning or discussion concerning the Deity'; Richard Hooker defined 'theology' in English as 'the science of things divine'.

2. Western Origins and History of the Modern Practice: From the Bible to ...

Transcendence	In religion, transcendence refers to the aspect of God's nature and power which is wholly independent of (and removed from) the material universe. This is contrasted with immanence where God is fully present in the physical world and thus accessible to creatures in various ways. In religious experience transcendence is a state of being that has overcome the limitations of physical existence and by some definitions has also become independent of it.
Swami Niranjanananda	Swami Niranjanananda (Senior) born as Nitya Niranjan Ghosh, usually called by the shortened name of Niranjan, was one of the foremost monks of Ramakrishna Mission and was one of the direct monastic disciples of Ramakrishna. Swami Niranjanananda was one of those few disciples,whom Sri Ramakrishna termed as 'Nityasiddhas' or 'Ishwarakotis' - that is, souls who are ever perfect. [Swami Niranjanananda (Senior)is termed Senior since there was another Swami Niranjanananda (Junior) also known as Pandalai Maharaj, later in the Ramakrishna Mission who died in 1972].
Swami Vivekananda	Swami Vivekananda was an Indian Hindu monk. He was a key figure in the introduction of Indian philosophies of Vedanta and Yoga to the western world, and was credited with raising interfaith awareness, bringing Hinduism to the status of a major world religion in the late 19th century. He was a major force in the revival of Hinduism in India, and contributed to the notion of nationalism in colonial India.
Daoism	In English, the words Daoism and Taoism are the subject of an ongoing controversy over the preferred romanization for naming this native Chinese philosophy and Chinese religion. The root Chinese word é" 'way, path' is romanized tao in the older Wade-Giles system and dào in the modern Pinyin system. The sometimes heated arguments over Taoism vs. Daoism involve sinology, phonemes, loanwords, and politics - not to mention whether Taoism should be pronounced or .
Caste	A caste is a combined social system of occupation, endogamy, culture, social class, and political power. caste should not be confused with class, in that members of a caste are deemed to be alike in function or culture, whereas not all members of a defined class may be so alike. Although Indian society is often now associated with the word 'caste', it was first used by the Portuguese to describe inherited class status in their own European society.
Tantra	Tantra and the universe is regarded as the divine play of Shakti and Shiva. The word Tantra also applies to any of the scriptures (called 'Tantras') commonly identified with the worship of Shakti. Tantra deals primarily with spiritual practices and ritual forms of worship, which aim at liberation from ignorance and rebirth.
Yoga	Yoga refers to traditional physical and mental disciplines that originated in India. The word is associated with meditative practices in Hinduism, Buddhism and Jainism.

2. Western Origins and History of the Modern Practice: From the Bible to ...

43

Perennial philosophy	Perennial philosophy is the notion of the universal recurrence of philosophical insight independent of epoch or culture, including universal truths on the nature of reality, humanity or consciousness (anthropological universals). The perennial philosophy is a perspective within the philosophy of religion which views each of the world's religious traditions as sharing a single, universal truth and a single divine foundation of all religious knowledge. Each world religion, independent of its cultural or historical context, is simply a different interpretation of this knowledge.
Rumi	Jalal ad-Din Mu?ammad Balkhi, also known as Jalal ad-Din Mu?ammad Rumi and popularly known as Mevlana in Turkey and Mawlana in Iran and Afghanistan but known to the English-speaking world simply as Rumi was a 13th-century Persian Muslim poet, jurist, theologian, and Sufi mystic. Rumi is a descriptive name meaning 'Roman' since he lived most of his life in an area called 'Rûm' (then under the control of Seljuq dynasty) because it was once ruled by the Eastern Roman Empire. He was one of the figures who flourished in the Sultanate of Rum.
Huston Cummings Smith	Huston Cummings Smith is a religious studies scholar in the United States. His book The World's Religions, remains a popular introduction to comparative religion. Smith was born in Soochow, China to Methodist missionaries and spent his first 17 years there.
Sufi	The lexical root of Sufi is variously traced to ØµÙÙˆÙ áʹ£Å«f 'wool', referring either to the simple cloaks the early Muslim ascetics wore, or possibly to ØµÙŽÙˆØ§§ áʹ£afÄ 'purity'. The two were combined by al-Rudhabari who said, 'The Sufi is the one who wears wool on top of purity.' The wool cloaks were sometimes a designation of their initiation into the Sufi order. The early Sufi orders considered the wearing of this coat an imitation of Isa bin Maryam (Jesus).
Constructivism	In the philosophy of mathematics, constructivism asserts that it is necessary to find a mathematical object to prove that it exists. When one assumes that an object does not exist and derives a contradiction from that assumption, one still has not found the object and therefore not proved its existence, according to constructivism. This viewpoint involves a verificational interpretation of the existence quantifier, which is at odds with its classical interpretation.
Kwame Anthony Appiah	Kwame Anthony Appiah is a Ghanaian-British-American philosopher, cultural theorist, and novelist whose interests include political and moral theory, the philosophy of language and mind, and African intellectual history. Kwame Anthony Appiah grew up in Ghana and earned a Ph.D. at Cambridge University. He is currently the Laurance S. Rockefeller University Professor of Philosophy at Princeton University.
Contextualism	Contextualism describes a collection of views in philosophy which emphasize the context in which an action, utterance, or expression occurs, and argues that, in some important respect, the action, utterance, or expression can only be understood relative to that context.

2. Western Origins and History of the Modern Practice: From the Bible to ...

	Contextualist views hold that philosophically controversial concepts, such as 'meaning P,' 'knowing that P,' 'having a reason to A,' and possibly even 'being true' or 'being right' only have meaning relative to a specified context. Some philosophers hold that context-dependence may lead to relativism; nevertheless, contextualist views are increasingly popular within philosophy.
Cosmogony	Cosmogony is any scientific theory concerning the coming into existence, or origin, of the cosmos or universe, or about how what sentient beings perceive as 'reality' came to be. The word comes from the Greek κοσμογον?α or κοσμογεν?α and the root of γ?(γ)νομαι / γ?γονα . In astronomy, cosmogony refers to the study of the origin of particular astrophysical objects or systems, and is most commonly used in reference to the origin of the solar system.
Cosmopolitanism	Cosmopolitanism is the ideology that all human ethnic groups belong to a single community based on a shared morality. Cosmopolitanism may entail some sort of world government or it may simply refer to more inclusive moral, economic, and/or political relationships between nations or individuals of different nations. A person who adheres to the idea of cosmopolitanism in any of its forms is called a cosmopolitan or cosmopolite.
Skepticism	Skepticism, but generally refers to any questioning attitude towards knowledge, facts, or opinions/beliefs stated as facts, or doubt regarding claims that are taken for granted elsewhere. The word may characterize a position on a single matter, as in the case of religious skepticism, which is 'doubt concerning basic religious principles (such as immortality, providence, and revelation)', but philosophical skepticism is an overall approach that requires all information to be well supported by evidence. Skeptics may even doubt the reliability of their own senses.

1. _____ was a prominent Theosophist, women's rights activist, writer and orator and supporter of Irish and Indian self rule.

   She was married at 19 to Frank Besant but separated from him over religious differences. Moving to London, she became a prominent speaker for the National Secular Society and writer and a close friend of Charles Bradlaugh.

   a. Henryk Batuta hoax
   b. Contemplation
   c. Creative visualization
   d. Annie Besant

2. . A _____ is a literary figure of speech that describes a subject by asserting that it is, on some point of comparison, the same as another otherwise unrelated object.

_____ is a type of analogy and is closely related to other rhetorical figures of speech that achieve their effects via association, comparison or resemblance including allegory, hyperbole, and simile.

One of the most prominent examples of a _____ in English literature is the All the world's a stage monologue from As You Like It:All the world's a stage,And all the men and women merely players;They have their exits and their entrances; -- William Shakespeare, As You Like It, 2/7

This quote is a _____ because the world is not literally a stage.

a. Metaphor
b. Metonymy
c. Mistakes were made
d. Nimism

3. _____ is the building and maintaining of colonies in one territory by people based elsewhere. _____ is a process whereby sovereignty over the colony is claimed by the metropole, who impose a new government and perhaps a new social structure and economy. _____ comprises unequal relationships between metropole and colony and between colonists and the indigenous population.

a. Colonialism
b. Abel Rey
c. Jean Reynaud
d. Pierre A. Riffard

4. File:Religious syms.svg _____ is the academic field of multi-disciplinary, secular study of religious beliefs, behaviors, and institutions. It describes, compares, interprets, and explains religion, emphasising systematic, historically-based, and cross-cultural perspectives.

While theology attempts to understand the intentions of a supernatural force (such as deities), _____ tries to study human religious behavior and belief from outside any particular religious viewpoint.

a. ADD model
b. Abel Rey
c. Jean Reynaud
d. Religious studies

5. . _____ is the title of a series of philosophical aphorisms by William Blake, written in 1788. Following on from his initial experiments with relief etching in the non-textual The Approach of Doom (1787), _____ and There is No Natural Religion represent Blake's first successful attempt to combine image and text via relief etching, and are thus the earliest of his illuminated manuscripts. As such, they serve as a significant milestone in Blake's career; as Peter Ackroyd points out, 'his newly invented form now changed the nature of his expression. It had enlarged his range; with relief etching, the words inscribed like those of God upon the tables of law, Blake could acquire a new role.'

2. Western Origins and History of the Modern Practice: From the Bible to ...

CHAPTER QUIZ: KEY TERMS, PEOPLE, PLACES, CONCEPTS

In 1822, Blake completed a short two-page dramatic piece which would prove to be the last of his illuminated manuscripts, entitled The Ghost of Abel A Revelation In the Visions of Jehovah Seen by William Blake.

a. Anagoge
b. Angel of the Lord
c. All Religions are One
d. Aseity

1. d

2. a

3. a

4. d

5. c

You can take the complete Chapter Practice Test

for 2. Western Origins and History of the Modern Practice: From the Bible to ...
on all key terms, persons, places, and concepts.

Online 99 Cents

http://www.JustTheFacts101.com

Use www.JustTheFacts101.com for all your study needs

including Facts101's online interactive problem solving labs in

chemistry, statistics, mathematics, and more.

3. The Skill of Reflexivity and Some Key Categories: The Terms of Our Tim

CHAPTER OUTLINE: KEY TERMS, PEOPLE, PLACES, CONCEPTS

	Bruno Latour
	History of religions
	Magic
	Miracles
	Religious experience
	Theory
	Perennial philosophy
	Perspective
	Initiation
	Plato
	Republic
	Perception
	EPIC
	Equality
	Reflexivity
	Humanities
	Friedrich
	Nietzsche
	Enlightenment
	Protestantism
	Colonialism

Freedom of religion

Modernity

Ayatollah

Quran

Expression

Piety

Secularism

World Religions

Violence

Rudolf Otto

Election

Metaphor

Myth and ritual

Theology

Merton Thesis

Mysticism

Philosophical analysis

Huston Cummings Smith

Rationalism

Radhakrishnan

Sufi

3. The Skill of Reflexivity and Some Key Categories: The Terms of Our Tim ...

51

CHAPTER OUTLINE: KEY TERMS, PEOPLE, PLACES, CONCEPTS

	Gospel
	Attitude
	Italian Renaissance
	Isaac Newton
	Renaissance
	Royal Society
	Agnosticism
	Alchemy
	Skepticism

CHAPTER HIGHLIGHTS & NOTES: KEY TERMS, PEOPLE, PLACES, CONCEPTS

Bruno Latour	Bruno Latour is a French sociologist of science and anthropologist and an influential theorist in the field of Science and Technology Studies (STS). After teaching at the École des Mines de Paris (Centre de Sociologie de l'Innovation) from 1982 to 2006, he is now Professor and vice-president for research at Sciences Po Paris (2007), where he is associated with the Centre de sociologie des organisations (CSO).
	He is best known for his books We Have Never Been Modern, Laboratory Life (with Steve Woolgar, 1979) and Science in Action (1987).
History of religions	The history of religion refers to the written record of human religious experiences and ideas. This period of religious history begins with the invention of writing about 5,000 years ago (3,000 BCE) in the Near East. The prehistory of religion relates to a study of religious beliefs that existed prior to the advent of written records. The timeline of religion is a comparative chronology of religion.
	The word 'religion' as it is used today does not have an obvious pre-colonial translation into non-European languages. Daniel Dubuisson writes that 'what the West and the history of religions in its wake have objectified under the name 'religion' is ...

Magic	Magic (sometimes referred to as stage magic to distinguish it from paranormal or ritual magic) is a performing art that entertains audiences by staging tricks or creating illusions of seemingly impossible or supernatural feats using natural means. These feats are called magic tricks, effects, or illusions. One who performs such illusions is called a magician or an illusionist.
Miracles	Thomas Paine, one of the Founding Fathers of the American Revolution, wrote 'All the tales of Miracles with which the Old and New Testament are filled, are fit only for impostors to preach and fools to believe'. Thomas Jefferson, principle author of the Declaration of Independence, edited a version of the Bible in which he removed sections of the New Testament containing supernatural aspects as well as perceived misinterpretations he believed had been added by the Four Evangelists. Jefferson wrote, 'The establishment of the innocent and genuine character of this benevolent moralist, and the rescuing it from the imputation of imposture, which has resulted from artificial systems, [footnote: e.g. The immaculate conception of Jesus, his deification, the creation of the world by him, his miraculous powers, his resurrection and visible ascension, his corporeal presence in the Eucharist, the Trinity; original sin, atonement, regeneration, election, orders of Hierarchy, etc.
Religious experience	A religious experience is a subjective experience in which an individual reports contact with a transcendent reality, an encounter or union with the divine. Such an experience often involves arriving at some knowledge or insight previously unavailable to the subject yet unaccountable or unforseeable according to the usual conceptual or psychological framework within which the subject has been used to operating. Religious experience generally brings understanding, partial or complete, of issues of a fundamental character that may have been a cause (whether consciously ackowledged or not) of anguish or alienation to the subject for an extended period of time.
Theory	In mathematical logic, a theory (also called a formal theory) is a set of sentences in a formal language. Usually a deductive system is understood from context. An element $\phi \in T$ of a theory T is then called an axiom of the theory, and any sentence that follows from the axioms ($T \vdash \phi$) is called a theorem of the theory.
Perennial philosophy	Perennial philosophy is the notion of the universal recurrence of philosophical insight independent of epoch or culture, including universal truths on the nature of reality, humanity or consciousness (anthropological universals). The perennial philosophy is a perspective within the philosophy of religion which views each of the world's religious traditions as sharing a single, universal truth and a single divine foundation of all religious knowledge. Each world religion, independent of its cultural or historical context, is simply a different interpretation of this knowledge.

3. The Skill of Reflexivity and Some Key Categories: The Terms of Our Tim ...

53

Perspective	Perspective in theory of cognition is the choice of a context or a reference from which to sense, categorize, measure or codify experience, cohesively forming a coherent belief, typically for comparing with another. One may further recognize a number of subtly distinctive meanings, close to those of paradigm, point of view, reality tunnel, umwelt, or weltanschauung. To choose a perspective is to choose a value system and, unavoidably, an associated belief system.
Initiation	Initiation is a concept in Theosophy that there are ten levels of spiritual development that beings who live on Earth can progress upward through. Within these levels, there are four basic levels of spiritual development that human beings on Earth progress through as they reincarnate, although evil acts may cause bad karma which may cause one to temporarily regress. These first four stages are identical to the four stages of enlightenment in Buddhism.
Plato	Plato was a Classical Greek philosopher, mathematician, student of Socrates, writer of philosophical dialogues, and founder of the Academy in Athens, the first institution of higher learning in the Western world. Along with his mentor, Socrates, and his student, Aristotle, Plato helped to lay the foundations of Western philosophy and science. In the words of A. N. Whitehead:' The safest general characterization of the European philosophical tradition is that it consists of a series of footnotes to Plato.'
Republic	A republic is a state under a form of government in which the people, or some significant portion of them, retain supreme control over the government. The term is generally also understood to describe a state where most decisions are made with reference to established laws, rather than the discretion of a head of state, and therefore monarchy is today generally considered to be incompatible with being a republic. One common modern definition of a republic is a state without a monarch.
Perception	Perception is the organization, identification, and interpretation of sensory information in order to fabricate a mental representation through the process of transduction, which sensors in the body transform signals from the environment into encoded neural signals. All perception involves signals in the nervous system, which in turn result from physical stimulation of the sense organs. For example, vision involves light striking the retinas of the eyes, smell is mediated by odor molecules and hearing involves pressure waves.
EPIC	EPIC (Executive-Process/Interactive Control) is a cognitive architecture developed by Professors David E. Kieras and David E. Meyer at the University of Michigan . EPIC has components that emulate various parts of the human-information processing system. Among these components are tools for perceptual, cognitive, and motor processing.

3. The Skill of Reflexivity and Some Key Categories: The Terms of Our Tim ...

Equality	Loosely, equality is the state of being quantitatively the same. More formally, equality is the binary relation on a set X defined by $\{(x, x) \mid x \in X\}$. The identity relation is the archetype of the more general concept of an equivalence relation on a set: those binary relations which are reflexive, symmetric, and transitive. The relation of equality is also antisymmetric.
Reflexivity	Reflexivity refers to circular relationships between cause and effect. A reflexive relationship is bidirectional with both the cause and the effect affecting one another in a situation that does not render both functions causes and effects. In sociology, reflexivity therefore comes to mean an act of self-reference where examination or action 'bends back on', refers to, and affects the entity instigating the action or examination.
Humanities	The humanities are academic disciplines that study the human condition, using methods that are primarily analytical, critical, or speculative, as distinguished from the mainly empirical approaches of the natural sciences. The humanities include ancient and modern languages, literature, history, philosophy, religion, and visual and performing arts such as music and theatre. The humanities that are also regarded as social sciences include technology, history, anthropology, area studies, communication studies, cultural studies, law and linguistics.
Friedrich	The Friedrich are the most ancient German-Bohemian glass-maker family. History From as early as 750 years ago, the shadowy picture of the oldest German-Bohemian glass-maker family Friedrich emerges, who contributed greatly towards the creation of the world-famous Bohemian glass (also called Bohemian Crystal). In pre-Hussite times they produced amazing works of vitreous art near Daubitz, nowadays called Doubice.
Nietzsche	Friedrich Wilhelm Nietzsche was a 19th-century German philosopher and classical philologist. He wrote critical texts on religion, morality, contemporary culture, philosophy and science, using a distinctive German-language style and displaying a fondness for metaphor, irony and aphorism. Nietzsche's influence remains substantial within and beyond philosophy, notably in existentialism and postmodernism.

Enlightenment	Enlightenment in a secular context often means the 'full comprehension of a situation', but in spiritual terms the word alludes to a spiritual revelation or deep insight into the meaning and purpose of all things, communication with or understanding of the mind of God, profound spiritual understanding or a fundamentally changed consciousness whereby everything is perceived as a unity. Some scientists believe that during meditative states leading up to the subjective experience of enlightenment there are actual physical changes in the brain. Buddhism The English term 'enlightenment' has commonly been used to translate several Sanskrit, Pali, Chinese and Japanese terms and concepts, especially bodhi, prajna, kensho, satori and buddhahood.
Protestantism	Protestantism is a branch within Christianity, containing many denominations of different practices and doctrines, that originated in the sixteenth-century Protestant Reformation. It is considered to be one of the primary divisions within the original Christian church, i.e., the Catholic Church, along with Eastern Orthodoxy. Some groups that are often loosely labeled 'Protestant' do not use the term to define themselves, and some tend to reject it because of the implication of being non-traditional.
Colonialism	Colonialism is the building and maintaining of colonies in one territory by people based elsewhere. Colonialism is a process whereby sovereignty over the colony is claimed by the metropole, who impose a new government and perhaps a new social structure and economy. Colonialism comprises unequal relationships between metropole and colony and between colonists and the indigenous population.
Freedom of religion	Freedom of religion is a principle that supports the freedom of an individual or community, in public or private, to manifest religion or belief in teaching, practice, worship, and observance; the concept is generally recognized also to include the freedom to change religion or not to follow any religion. Freedom of religion is considered by many people and nations to be a fundamental human right. Thomas Jefferson once said 'among the inestimable of our blessings, also, is that ...of liberty to worship our Creator in the way we think most agreeable to His will; ...' In a country with a state religion, Freedom of religion is generally considered to mean that the government permits religious practices of other sects besides the state religion, and does not persecute believers in other faiths.
Modernity	Modernity typically refers to a post-traditional, post-medieval historical period, one marked by the move from feudalism (or agrarianism) toward capitalism, industrialization, secularization, rationalization, the nation-state and its constituent institutions and forms of surveillance (Barker 2005, 444). Conceptually, modernity relates to the modern era and to modernism, but forms a distinct concept.

Ayatollah	Ayatollah is a high-ranking title given to Usuli Twelver Shi'ah clerics. Those who carry the title are experts in Islamic studies such as jurisprudence, ethics, and philosophy and usually teach in Islamic seminaries. The next lower clerical rank is Hojatoleslam wal-muslemin.
Quran	The Quran, also transliterated Qur'an, Koran, Al-Coran, Coran, Kuran, and Al-Qur'an, is the central religious text of Islam, which Muslims consider the verbatim word of God . It is regarded widely as the finest piece of literature in the Arabic language. The Quran is composed of verses (Ayah) that make up 114 chapters (suras) of unequal length which are classified either as Meccan or Medinan depending upon the place and time of their claimed revelation.
Expression	In mathematics, an expression is a finite combination of symbols that is well-formed according to rules that depend on the context. Symbols can designate numbers (constants), variables, operations, functions, and other mathematical symbols, as well as punctuation, symbols of grouping, and other syntactic symbols. The use of expressions can range from the simple: $0 + 0$ to the complex: $$f(a) + \sum_{k=1}^{n} \frac{1}{k!} \frac{d^k}{dt^k}\bigg|_{t=0} f(u(t)) + \int_0^1 \frac{(1-t)^n}{n!} \frac{d^{n+1}}{dt^{n+1}} f(u(t))\, dt.$$ We can think of algebraic expressions as generalizations of common arithmetic operations that are formed by combining numbers, variables, and mathematical operations.
Piety	In spiritual terminology, piety is a virtue that can mean religious devotion, spirituality, or a combination of both. A common element in most conceptions of piety is humility. The word piety comes from the Latin word pietas, the noun form of the adjective pius (which means 'devout' or 'good').
Secularism	Secularism is the principle of separation between government institutions and the persons mandated to represent the State from religious institutions and religious dignitaries. In one sense, secularism may assert the right to be free from religious rule and teachings, and the right to freedom from governmental imposition of religion upon the people within a state that is neutral on matters of belief. In another sense, it refers to the view that human activities and decisions, especially political ones, should be unbiased by religious influence.
World Religions	World Religions was an educational television show which was produced and broadcast by TVOntario (known at the time as the Ontario Educational Communications Authority) in 1973.

3. The Skill of Reflexivity and Some Key Categories: The Terms of Our Tim ...

57

CHAPTER HIGHLIGHTS & NOTES: KEY TERMS, PEOPLE, PLACES, CONCEPTS

	The three episode names known are:•'Judaism'•'Who Do Men Say That I Am?'•'Islam: Terrorists or Visionaries' All episodes were 30 minutes in length.
Violence	Violence is defined by the World Health Organization as the intentional use of physical force or power, threatened or actual, against oneself, another person, or against a group or community, that either results in or has a high likelihood of resulting in injury, death, psychological harm, maldevelopment or deprivation. This definition associates intentionality with the committing of the act itself, irrespective of the outcome it produces. Globally, violence takes the lives of more than 1.5 million people annually: just over 50% due to suicide, some 35% due to homicide, and just over 12% as a direct result of war or some other form of conflict.
Rudolf Otto	Rudolf Otto was an eminent German Lutheran theologian and scholar of comparative religion. Born in Peine near Hanover, Otto attended the Gymnasium Andreanum in Hildesheim and studied at the universities of Erlangen and Göttingen, where he wrote his dissertation on Martin Luther's understanding of the Holy Spirit, and his habilitation on Kant. By 1906, he held a position as extraordinary professor, and in 1910 he received an honorary doctorate from the University of Giessen.
Election	An election is a formal decision-making process by which a population chooses an individual to hold public office. Elections have been the usual mechanism by which modern representative democracy has operated since the 17th century. Elections may fill offices in the legislature, sometimes in the executive and judiciary, and for regional and local government.
Metaphor	A metaphor is a literary figure of speech that describes a subject by asserting that it is, on some point of comparison, the same as another otherwise unrelated object. Metaphor is a type of analogy and is closely related to other rhetorical figures of speech that achieve their effects via association, comparison or resemblance including allegory, hyperbole, and simile. One of the most prominent examples of a metaphor in English literature is the All the world's a stage monologue from As You Like It:All the world's a stage,And all the men and women merely players;They have their exits and their entrances; -- William Shakespeare, As You Like It, 2/7 This quote is a metaphor because the world is not literally a stage.
Myth and ritual	In traditional societies, Myth and ritual are two central components of religious practice.

3. The Skill of Reflexivity and Some Key Categories: The Terms of Our Tim ...

CHAPTER HIGHLIGHTS & NOTES: KEY TERMS, PEOPLE, PLACES, CONCEPTS

	Although Myth and ritual are commonly united as parts of religion, the exact relationship between them has been a matter of controversy among scholars. One of the approaches to this problem is 'the Myth and ritual, or myth-ritualist, theory', which holds that 'myth does not stand by itself but is tied to ritual'.
Theology	Theology is the rational and systematic study of religion and its influences and of the nature of religious truth, or the learned profession acquired by specialized courses in religion, usually taught at a college or seminary. Augustine of Hippo defined the Latin equivalent, theologia, as 'reasoning or discussion concerning the Deity'; Richard Hooker defined 'theology' in English as 'the science of things divine'. The term can, however, be used for a variety of different disciplines or forms of discourse.
Merton Thesis	The Merton Thesis is an argument about the nature of early experimental science proposed by Robert K. Merton. Similar to Max Weber's famous claim on the link between Protestant ethic and the capitalist economy, Merton argued for a similar positive correlation between the rise of Protestant pietism and early experimental science. The Merton Thesis has resulted in continuous debates.
Mysticism	Mysticism is the pursuit of communion with, identity with divinity, spiritual truth intuition, instinct or insight. Mysticism usually centers on a practice or practices intended to nurture those experiences or awareness. Mysticism may be dualistic, maintaining a distinction between the self and the divine, or may be nondualistic.
Philosophical analysis	Philosophical analysis is a general term for techniques typically used by philosophers in the analytic tradition that involve 'breaking down' (i.e. analyzing) philosophical issues.
Huston Cummings Smith	Huston Cummings Smith is a religious studies scholar in the United States. His book The World's Religions, remains a popular introduction to comparative religion. Smith was born in Soochow, China to Methodist missionaries and spent his first 17 years there.
Rationalism	Rationalism in politics is often seen as the midpoint in the three major political viewpoints of realism, rationalism, and internationalism. Whereas Realism and Internationalism are both on ends of the scale, rationalism tends to occupy the middle ground on most issues, and finds compromise between these two conflicting points of view. Believers of Rationalism believe that multinational and multilateral organizations have their place in the world order, but not that a world government would be feasible.
Radhakrishnan	Sarvepalli Radhakrishnan, OM, FBA, (Telugu: à°¸à°°à±à°µà±à°ªà°²à±à°²à°¿ à°°à°¾à°§à°¾à°•à±ƒà°·à±à°£à±); (5 September 1888 - 17 April 1975), was an Indian philosopher and statesman.

3. The Skill of Reflexivity and Some Key Categories: The Terms of Our Tim ...

59

	He was the first Vice-President of India (1952-1962), and its second President (1962-1967). One of India's most influential scholars of comparative religion and philosophy, Radhakrishnan is considered through his efforts to have built a bridge between East and West by having shown the philosophical systems of each tradition to be comprehensible within the terms of the other.
Sufi	The lexical root of Sufi is variously traced to ØµÙÙˆÙ á¹£Å«f 'wool', referring either to the simple cloaks the early Muslim ascetics wore, or possibly to ØµÙŽÙØ§ á¹£afÄ 'purity'. The two were combined by al-Rudhabari who said, 'The Sufi is the one who wears wool on top of purity.' The wool cloaks were sometimes a designation of their initiation into the Sufi order. The early Sufi orders considered the wearing of this coat an imitation of Isa bin Maryam (Jesus).
Gospel	A Gospel is a writing that describes the life of Jesus. The word is primarily used to refer to the four canonical Gospels: the Gospel of Matthew, Gospel of Mark, Gospel of Luke and Gospel of John, probably written between AD 65 and 80. They appear to have been originally untitled; they were quoted anonymously in the first half of the second century (i.e. 100-150) but the names by which they are currently known appear suddenly around the year 180. The first canonical Gospel written is thought by most scholars to be Mark (c 65-70), which was according to the majority used as a source for the Gospels of Matthew and Luke.
Attitude	Attitude as a term of fine art refers to the posture or gesture given to a figure by a painter or sculptor. It applies to the body and not to a mental state, but the arrangement of the body is presumed to serve a communicative or expressive purpose. An example of a conventional attitude in art is proskynesis to indicate respect toward God, emperors, clerics of high status, and religious icons; in Byzantine art, it is particularly characteristic in depictions of the emperor paying homage to Christ.
Italian Renaissance	The Italian Renaissance was the earliest manifestation of the general European Renaissance, a period of great cultural change and achievement that began in Italy around the end of the 13th century and lasted until the 16th century, marking the transition between Medieval and Early Modern Europe. The term Renaissance is in essence a modern one that came into currency in the 19th century, in the work of historians such as Jacob Burckhardt. Although the origins of a movement that was confined largely to the literate culture of intellectual endeavor and patronage can be traced to the earlier part of the 14th century, many aspects of Italian culture and society remained largely Medieval; the Renaissance did not come into full swing until the end of the century.
Isaac Newton	Sir Isaac Newton PRS MP (25 December 1642 - 20 March 1727

[NS: 4 January 1643 - 31 March 1727]) was an English physicist, mathematician, astronomer, natural philosopher, alchemist, and theologian, who has been 'considered by many to be the greatest and most influential scientist who ever lived.' His monograph Philosophiæ Naturalis Principia Mathematica, published in 1687, lays the foundations for most of classical mechanics. In this work, Newton described universal gravitation and the three laws of motion, which dominated the scientific view of the physical universe for the next three centuries. Newton showed that the motions of objects on Earth and of celestial bodies are governed by the same set of natural laws, by demonstrating the consistency between Kepler's laws of planetary motion and his theory of gravitation, thus removing the last doubts about heliocentrism and advancing the Scientific Revolution.

Renaissance	The Renaissance was a cultural movement that spanned the period roughly from the 14th to the 17th century, beginning in Italy in the Late Middle Ages and later spreading to the rest of Europe. Though the invention of printing sped the dissemination of ideas from the later 15th century, the changes of the Renaissance were not uniformly experienced across Europe. As a cultural movement, it encompassed innovative flowering of Latin and vernacular literatures, beginning with the 14th-century resurgence of learning based on classical sources, which contemporaries credited to Petrarch, the development of linear perspective and other techniques of rendering a more natural reality in painting, and gradual but widespread educational reform.
Royal Society	The Royal Society of London for the Improvement of Natural Knowledge, known simply as the Royal Society is a learned society for science that was founded in 1660 and is considered by most to be the oldest such society still in existence. Although a charitable body, it serves as the Academy of Sciences of the United Kingdom . Fellowship, granted for life, is awarded to scientists after their election by existing fellows, and is considered a great honour.
Agnosticism	Agnosticism is the view that the truth values of certain claims--especially claims about the existence or non-existence of any deity, but also other religious and metaphysical claims--are unknown or unknowable. Agnosticism can be defined in various ways, and is sometimes used to indicate doubt or a skeptical approach to questions. In some senses, agnosticism is a stance about the difference between belief and knowledge, rather than about any specific claim or belief.
Alchemy	Alchemy, refers to a medieval quest for an elixir or kimia capable of turning copper and other base metals to gold. Alchemy is both a philosophy and an ancient practice focused on the attempt to accomplish this transmutation, investigating the preparation of the 'elixir of longevity', and achieving ultimate wisdom, involving the improvement of the alchemist as well as the making of several substances described as possessing unusual properties. The practical aspect of alchemy can be viewed as a protoscience, having generated the basics of modern inorganic chemistry, namely concerning procedures, equipment and the identification and use of many current substances.
Skepticism	Skepticism, but generally refers to any questioning attitude towards knowledge, facts, or opinions/beliefs stated as facts, or doubt regarding claims that are taken for granted elsewhere.

3. The Skill of Reflexivity and Some Key Categories: The Terms of Our Tim ...

61

The word may characterize a position on a single matter, as in the case of religious skepticism, which is 'doubt concerning basic religious principles (such as immortality, providence, and revelation)', but philosophical skepticism is an overall approach that requires all information to be well supported by evidence. Skeptics may even doubt the reliability of their own senses.

CHAPTER QUIZ: KEY TERMS, PEOPLE, PLACES, CONCEPTS

1. Sarvepalli _____, OM, FBA, (Telugu: à°¸à°°à±±à°ªà±‡à°°à±±à°²à±à°¿ à°°à°¾à°§à°¾à°•à±•à±ƒà±•à±à°²à°£); (5 September 1888 - 17 April 1975), was an Indian philosopher and statesman. He was the first Vice-President of India (1952-1962), and its second President (1962-1967).

   One of India's most influential scholars of comparative religion and philosophy, _____ is considered through his efforts to have built a bridge between East and West by having shown the philosophical systems of each tradition to be comprehensible within the terms of the other.

   a. Zeno of Citium
   b. Radhakrishnan
   c. Mahmud of Ghazni
   d. Liu Bang

2. The _____(s) refers to the written record of human religious experiences and ideas. This period of religious history begins with the invention of writing about 5,000 years ago (3,000 BCE) in the Near East. The pre_____(s) relates to a study of religious beliefs that existed prior to the advent of written records. The timeline of religion is a comparative chronology of religion.

   The word 'religion' as it is used today does not have an obvious pre-colonial translation into non-European languages. Daniel Dubuisson writes that 'what the West and the _____ in its wake have objectified under the name 'religion' is ... something quite unique, which could be appropriate only to itself and its own history.' The history of other cultures' interaction with the religious category is therefore their interaction with an idea that first developed in Europe under the influence of Christianity.

   a. Society of Jewish Ethics
   b. Albert Lautman
   c. Antoine Le Grand
   d. History of religions

3. . _____ is the organization, identification, and interpretation of sensory information in order to fabricate a mental representation through the process of transduction, which sensors in the body transform signals from the environment into encoded neural signals.

3. The Skill of Reflexivity and Some Key Categories: The Terms of Our Tim ...

All _____ involves signals in the nervous system, which in turn result from physical stimulation of the sense organs. For example, vision involves light striking the retinas of the eyes, smell is mediated by odor molecules and hearing involves pressure waves.

a. Perceptual learning
b. Reconstructive observation
c. Perception
d. Thought experiment

4. In mathematical logic, a _____ (also called a formal _____) is a set of sentences in a formal language. Usually a deductive system is understood from context. An element $\phi \in T$ of a _____ T is then called an axiom of the _____, and any sentence that follows from the axioms ($T \vdash \phi$) is called a theorem of the _____.

a. Theory of pure equality
b. Religious identity
c. Religious views on organ donation
d. Theory

5. _____ (Executive-Process/Interactive Control) is a cognitive architecture developed by Professors David E. Kieras and David E. Meyer at the University of Michigan .

_____ has components that emulate various parts of the human-information processing system. Among these components are tools for perceptual, cognitive, and motor processing.

a. EPIC
b. Soar
c. Self-evidence
d. Thought experiment

1. b

2. d

3. c

4. d

5. a

You can take the complete Chapter Practice Test

for 3. The Skill of Reflexivity and Some Key Categories: The Terms of Our Tim ...
on all key terms, persons, places, and concepts.

Online 99 Cents

http://www.JustTheFacts101.com

Use www.JustTheFacts101.com for all your study needs

including Facts101's online interactive problem solving labs in

chemistry, statistics, mathematics, and more.

CHAPTER OUTLINE: KEY TERMS, PEOPLE, PLACES, CONCEPTS

	Iris Murdoch
	Cosmogony
	CoSMoS
	Mysticism
	Philosophical analysis
	Ernst Bergmann
	Plato
	Stoicism
	Logos
	Gospel
	Graf
	Mythologies
	Protestantism
	Myth and ritual
	Jerusalem
	Passover
	Creation myth
	Joseph Campbell
	EPIC
	Epic of Gilgamesh
	Hermes Trismegistus

_____ | Cicero

_____ | Civil religion

_____ | Renaissance

_____ | Expression

_____ | Piety

_____ | Violence

_____ | Hittites

_____ | Scapegoat

_____ | Herodotus

_____ | Oracle

_____ | Hippo

_____ | I Ching

_____ | Torah

_____ | Demon

_____ | Religious experience

_____ | Telepathy

_____ | Buddha

_____ | Bahubali

_____ | Asceticism

_____ | Friedrich

Iris Murdoch	Dame Iris Murdoch DBE (15 July 1919 - 8 February 1999) was an Irish-born British author and philosopher, best known for her novels about political and social questions of good and evil, sexual relationships, morality, and the power of the unconscious. Her first published novel, Under the Net, was selected in 1998 as one of Modern Library's 100 best English-language novels of the 20th century. In 1987, she was made a Dame Commander of the Order of the British Empire.
Cosmogony	Cosmogony is any scientific theory concerning the coming into existence, or origin, of the cosmos or universe, or about how what sentient beings perceive as 'reality' came to be. The word comes from the Greek κοσμογον?α or κοσμογεν?α and the root of γ?(γ)νομαι / γ?γονα . In astronomy, cosmogony refers to the study of the origin of particular astrophysical objects or systems, and is most commonly used in reference to the origin of the solar system.
CoSMoS	CoSMoS is a UK funded research project seeking do build capacity in generic modelling tools and simulation techniques for complex systems. Its acronym stands for Complex Systems Modelling and Simulation. This is a four-year project, running from 2007 to 2011 as a collaboration between the University of York and Kent, with further collaborations from the University of Abertay Dundee and Bristol Robotics Laboratory.
Mysticism	Mysticism is the pursuit of communion with, identity with divinity, spiritual truth intuition, instinct or insight. Mysticism usually centers on a practice or practices intended to nurture those experiences or awareness. Mysticism may be dualistic, maintaining a distinction between the self and the divine, or may be nondualistic.
Philosophical analysis	Philosophical analysis is a general term for techniques typically used by philosophers in the analytic tradition that involve 'breaking down' (i.e. analyzing) philosophical issues.
Ernst Bergmann	Ernst Bergmann (7 August 1881, Colditz, Kingdom of Saxony - 16 April 1945, Naumburg) was a German philosopher and proponent of Nazism. He studied philosophy and German philology at the University of Leipzig and got his PhD in 1905. Subsequently he continued his studies in Berlin. Later he returned to Leipzig, where he received the status of Privatdozent at the university in 1911. In 1916 he was awarded the position of Ausserordentlicher Professor (professor without chair).
Plato	Plato was a Classical Greek philosopher, mathematician, student of Socrates, writer of philosophical dialogues, and founder of the Academy in Athens, the first institution of higher learning in the Western world. Along with his mentor, Socrates, and his student, Aristotle, Plato helped to lay the foundations of Western philosophy and science. In the words of A. N. Whitehead:' The safest general characterization of the European philosophical tradition is that it consists of a series of footnotes to Plato.'

4. The Creative Functions of Myth and Ritual: Performing the World

Stoicism	Stoicism is a school of Hellenistic philosophy founded in Athens by Zeno of Citium in the early 3rd century BC. The Stoics taught that destructive emotions resulted from errors in judgment, and that a sage, or person of 'moral and intellectual perfection,' would not suffer such emotions.
	Stoics were concerned with the active relationship between cosmic determinism and human freedom, and the belief that it is virtuous to maintain a will (called prohairesis) that is in accord with nature.
Logos	Logos is an important term in philosophy, psychology, rhetoric, and religion. Originally a word meaning 'a ground', 'a plea', 'an opinion', 'an expectation', 'word,' 'speech,' 'account,' 'reason,' it became a technical term in philosophy, beginning with Heraclitus (ca. 535-475 BC), who used the term for a principle of order and knowledge.
	Ancient philosophers used the term in different ways.
Gospel	A Gospel is a writing that describes the life of Jesus. The word is primarily used to refer to the four canonical Gospels: the Gospel of Matthew, Gospel of Mark, Gospel of Luke and Gospel of John, probably written between AD 65 and 80. They appear to have been originally untitled; they were quoted anonymously in the first half of the second century (i.e. 100-150) but the names by which they are currently known appear suddenly around the year 180.
	The first canonical Gospel written is thought by most scholars to be Mark (c 65-70), which was according to the majority used as a source for the Gospels of Matthew and Luke.
Graf	Graf or Gräfin (female) is a historical German noble title equal in rank to a count or a British earl (an Anglo-Saxon title akin to the Viking title Jarl). A derivation ultimately from the Greek verb graphein 'to write' may be fanciful: Paul the Deacon wrote in Latin ca 790: 'the count of the Bavarians that they call gravio who governed Bauzanum and other strongholds...' (Historia Langobardorum, V.xxxvi); this may be read to make the term a Germanic one, but by then using Latin terms was quite common.
	Since August 1919, in Germany, Graf and all other titles are considered a part of the surname.
Mythologies	Mythologies is a book by Roland Barthes, published in 1957. It is a collection of essays taken from Les Lettres nouvelles, examining the tendency of contemporary social value systems to create modern myths. Barthes also looks at the semiology of the process of myth creation, updating Ferdinand de Saussure's system of sign analysis by adding a second level where signs are elevated to the level of myth. It is considered to be a key antecedent of cultural studies.
Protestantism	Protestantism is a branch within Christianity, containing many denominations of different practices and doctrines, that originated in the sixteenth-century Protestant Reformation.

	It is considered to be one of the primary divisions within the original Christian church, i.e., the Catholic Church, along with Eastern Orthodoxy. Some groups that are often loosely labeled 'Protestant' do not use the term to define themselves, and some tend to reject it because of the implication of being non-traditional.
Myth and ritual	In traditional societies, Myth and ritual are two central components of religious practice. Although Myth and ritual are commonly united as parts of religion, the exact relationship between them has been a matter of controversy among scholars. One of the approaches to this problem is 'the Myth and ritual, or myth-ritualist, theory', which holds that 'myth does not stand by itself but is tied to ritual'.
Jerusalem	Jerusalem is the title of a book written by Moses Mendelssohn, which was first published in 1783 - the same year, when the Prussian officer Christian Wilhelm von Dohm published the second part of his Mémoire Concerning the amelioration of the civil status of the Jews. Moses Mendelssohn was one of the key figures of Jewish Enlightenment (Haskalah) and his philosophical treatise, dealing with social contract and political theory (especially concerning the question of the separation between religion and state), can be regarded as his most important contribution to Haskalah. The book which was written in Prussia on the eve of the French Revolution, consisted of two parts and each one was paged separately.
Passover	Passover is a Jewish and Samaritan holy day and festival commemorating the Hebrews' escape from enslavement in Egypt. Passover begins on the 15th day of the month of Nisan , the first month of the Hebrew calendar's festival year according to the Hebrew Bible. In the story of the Exodus, the Bible tells that God inflicted ten plagues upon the Egyptians before Pharaoh would release his Hebrew slaves, with the tenth plague being the killing of all of the firstborn, from the Pharaoh's son to the firstborn of the dungeon captive, to the firstborn of cattle.
Creation myth	A creation myth is a symbolic narrative of a culture, tradition or people that describes their earliest beginnings, how the world they know began and how they first came into it. Creation myths develop in oral traditions, and are the most common form of myth, found throughout human culture. In the society in which it is told, a creation myth is usually regarded as conveying profound truths, although not necessarily in a historical or literal sense.
Joseph Campbell	Initiatives undertaken by the Joseph CampbellF include: The Collected Works of Joseph Campbell, a series of books and recordings that aims to pull together Campbell's myriad-minded work; the Erdman Campbell Award; the Mythological RoundTables, a network of local groups around the globe that explore the subjects of comparative mythology, psychology, religion and culture; and the collection of Campbell's library and papers housed at the OPUS Archive and Research Center .

	After Campbell's death, Jean Erdman and the Joseph Campbell Foundation donated his papers, books and other effects to the Center for the Study of Depth Psychology at Pacifica Graduate Institute in Carpinteria, California. The Center became the OPUS Archive and Research Center and is the home of the collection.
EPIC	EPIC (Executive-Process/Interactive Control) is a cognitive architecture developed by Professors David E. Kieras and David E. Meyer at the University of Michigan .
	EPIC has components that emulate various parts of the human-information processing system. Among these components are tools for perceptual, cognitive, and motor processing.
Epic of Gilgamesh	The Epic of Gilgamesh is an epic poem from Ancient Mesopotamia and is among the earliest known works of literary writings. Scholars believe that it originated as a series of Sumerian legends and poems about the mythological hero-king Gilgamesh, which were gathered into a longer Akkadian poem much later; the most complete version existing today is preserved on 12 clay tablets in the library collection of the 7th century BCE Assyrian king Ashurbanipal. It was originally titled He who Saw the Deep (Sha naqba Ä«muru) or Surpassing All Other Kings (ShÂ«tur eli sharrÄ«).
Hermes Trismegistus	MythologyHermes Trismegistus Â· Thoth Â· Poimandres
	HermeticaCorpus Hermeticum Â· Kybalion
	Three Parts of the Wisdom of the Whole UniverseAlchemy Â· Astrology Â· Theurgy
	Influence and Influences
	Hermetic MovementsRosicrucianism
	OrdersHermetic Order of the Golden Dawn Â· Hermetic Brotherhood of Luxor Â· Hermetic Brotherhood of Light
	Topics in HermetismQabalah Occult and divinatory tarot Hermetists and HermeticistsJohn Dee . Aleister Crowley Â· Israel RegardieThÄbit ibn Qurra Â· ParacelsusGiordano Bruno Â· Manly P. Hall Â· Samuel MacGregor Mathers Â· William WestcottFranz BardonHermes Trismegistus is the representation of the combination of the Greek god Hermes and the Egyptian god Thoth. In Hellenistic Egypt, the Greeks recognised the congruence of their God Hermes with the Egyptian god Thoth.
Cicero	Marcus Tullius Cicero was a Roman philosopher, statesman, lawyer, orator, political theorist, Roman consul and constitutionalist.

He came from a wealthy municipal family of the equestrian order, and is widely considered one of Rome's greatest orators and prose stylists.

He introduced the Romans to the chief schools of Greek philosophy and created a Latin philosophical vocabulary (with neologisms such as humanitas, qualitas, quantitas, and essentia) distinguishing himself as a linguist, translator, and philosopher.

Civil religion	The intended meaning of the term civil religion often varies according to whether one is a sociologist of religion or a professional political commentator. The following discussion includes both perspectives followed by a brief history of the concept. Within the contexts of the monotheistic, prophetic, revealed faiths, civil religion can be problematic from a theological perspective.
Renaissance	The Renaissance was a cultural movement that spanned the period roughly from the 14th to the 17th century, beginning in Italy in the Late Middle Ages and later spreading to the rest of Europe. Though the invention of printing sped the dissemination of ideas from the later 15th century, the changes of the Renaissance were not uniformly experienced across Europe. As a cultural movement, it encompassed innovative flowering of Latin and vernacular literatures, beginning with the 14th-century resurgence of learning based on classical sources, which contemporaries credited to Petrarch, the development of linear perspective and other techniques of rendering a more natural reality in painting, and gradual but widespread educational reform.
Expression	In mathematics, an expression is a finite combination of symbols that is well-formed according to rules that depend on the context. Symbols can designate numbers (constants), variables, operations, functions, and other mathematical symbols, as well as punctuation, symbols of grouping, and other syntactic symbols. The use of expressions can range from the simple: $0 + 0$ to the complex: $f(a) + \sum_{k=1}^{n} \frac{1}{k!} \frac{d^k}{dt^k}\bigg|_{t=0} f(u(t)) + \int_0^1 \frac{(1-t)^n}{n!} \frac{d^{n+1}}{dt^{n+1}} f(u(t))\, dt.$ We can think of algebraic expressions as generalizations of common arithmetic operations that are formed by combining numbers, variables, and mathematical operations.
Piety	In spiritual terminology, piety is a virtue that can mean religious devotion, spirituality, or a combination of both. A common element in most conceptions of piety is humility. The word piety comes from the Latin word pietas, the noun form of the adjective pius (which means 'devout' or 'good').

4. The Creative Functions of Myth and Ritual: Performing the World

Violence	Violence is defined by the World Health Organization as the intentional use of physical force or power, threatened or actual, against oneself, another person, or against a group or community, that either results in or has a high likelihood of resulting in injury, death, psychological harm, maldevelopment or deprivation. This definition associates intentionality with the committing of the act itself, irrespective of the outcome it produces. Globally, violence takes the lives of more than 1.5 million people annually: just over 50% due to suicide, some 35% due to homicide, and just over 12% as a direct result of war or some other form of conflict.
Hittites	Though heavily influenced by Mesopotamian mythology, the religion of the Hittites and Luwians retains noticeable Indo-European elements, for example Tarhunt the god of thunder, and his conflict with the serpent Illuyanka, which resembles, among other things, the conflict between Indra and the cosmic serpent Vrtra in Indo-Aryan mythology. Tarhunt has a son, Telepinu and a daughter, Inara. Inara is involved with the Puruli spring festival.
Scapegoat	In modern usage a scapegoat may be a child, employee, peer, ethnic or religious group, or country singled out for unmerited negative treatment or blame. A whipping boy or 'fall guy' is a form of scapegoat. Scapegoat derives from the common English translation of the Hebrew term azazel which occurs in Leviticus 16:8 after the prefix la- .
Herodotus	Herodotus of Halicarnassus was a Greek historian who lived in the 5th century BC . He is regarded as the 'Father of History' in Western culture. He was the first historian known to collect his materials systematically, test their accuracy to a certain extent and arrange them in a well-constructed and vivid narrative.
Oracle	An Oracle is a person or agency considered to be a source of wise counsel or prophetic opinion. It may also be a revealed prediction or precognition of the future, from deities, that is spoken through another object or life-form (e.g.: augury and auspice). In the ancient world many sites gained a reputation for the dispensing of oracular wisdom: they too became known as 'Oracles,' and the oracular utterances, called khrÄ"smoi in Greek, were often referred to under the same name--a name derived from the Latin verb ÅrÄre, to speak.
Hippo	Hippo was a Presocratic Greek philosopher. He is variously described as coming from Rhegium, Metapontum, Samos, and Croton, and it is possible that there was more than one philosopher with this name.

I Ching	The I Ching or 'Yì Jīng' (pinyin), also known as the Classic of Changes, Book of Changes and Zhouyi, is one of the oldest of the Chinese classic texts. The book contains a divination system comparable to Western geomancy or the West African Ifá system; in Western cultures and modern East Asia, it is still widely used for this purpose. Traditionally, the I Ching and its hexagrams were thought to pre-date recorded history, and based on traditional Chinese accounts, its origins trace back to the 3rd to the 2nd millennium BC. Modern scholarship suggests that the earliest layer of the text may date from the end of the 2nd millennium BC, but place doubts on the mythological aspects in the traditional accounts.
Torah	The term 'Torah' , refers either to the Five Books of Moses or to the entirety of Judaism's founding legal and ethical religious texts. A 'Sefer Torah' (×¡Öµ×¤Ö¶×¨ ×ªÖ¼×•×Ö¹×¨Ö¸×", 'book of Torah') or Torah scroll, is a copy of the Torah written on parchment in a formal, traditional manner by a specially trained scribe under very strict requirements. The Torah is the first of three parts of the Tanakh , the founding religious document of Judaism, Messiannic, and Hebrew belief, and is divided into five books, whose names in English are Genesis, Exodus, Leviticus, Numbers, and Deuteronomy, in reference to their themes .
Demon	A demon is a supernatural, often malevolent being prevalent in religion, occultism, literature, and folklore. The original Greek word daimon does not carry the negative connotation initially understood by implementation of the Koine δαιμ?νιον (daimonion), and later ascribed to any cognate words sharing the root. In Ancient Near Eastern religions as well as in the Abrahamic traditions, including ancient and medieval Christian demonology, a demon is considered an 'unclean spirit' which may cause demonic possession, calling for an exorcism.
Religious experience	A religious experience is a subjective experience in which an individual reports contact with a transcendent reality, an encounter or union with the divine. Such an experience often involves arriving at some knowledge or insight previously unavailable to the subject yet unnaccountable or unforseeable according to the usual conceptual or psychological framework within which the subject has been used to operating. Religious experience generally brings understanding, partial or complete, of issues of a fundamental character that may have been a cause (whether consciously ackowledged or not) of anguish or alienation to the subject for an extended period of time.
Telepathy	Telepathy , is the ostensible transfer of information on thoughts or feelings between individuals by means other than the five senses. The term was coined in 1882 by the classical scholar Fredric W. H. Myers, a founder of the Society for Psychical Research, specifically to replace the earlier expression thought-transference.

4. The Creative Functions of Myth and Ritual: Performing the World

Buddha	Usually Buddha refers to SiddhÄrtha Gautama , the historical founder of Buddhism, for this Buddha age, who adopted that title. He is sometimes referred to as Sakyamuni or The Buddha Gautama , in order to distinguish him from other Buddha s (cf. Buddha hood, enlightenment, nirvana.)
Bahubali	Bahubali also called Gomateshwara was a Jain Arihanta. According to Jainism he was the second of the hundred sons of the first Tirthankara, Rishabha and king of Podanpur. The Adipurana, a 10th century Kannada text by Jain poet Adikavi Pampa (fl. 941 CE), written in Champu style, a mix of prose and verse and spread over in sixteen cantos, deals with the ten lives of the first tirthankara, Rishabha and his two sons, Bharata and Bahubali.
Asceticism	Asceticism describes a lifestyle characterized by abstinence from various worldly pleasures, often with the aim of pursuing religious and spiritual goals. Many religious traditions (e.g. Buddhism, Jainism, the Christian desert fathers) include practices that involve restraint with respect to actions of body, speech, and mind. The founders and earliest practitioners of these religions lived extremely austere lifestyles, refraining from sensual pleasures and the accumulation of material wealth.
Friedrich	The Friedrich are the most ancient German-Bohemian glass-maker family. History From as early as 750 years ago, the shadowy picture of the oldest German-Bohemian glass-maker family Friedrich emerges, who contributed greatly towards the creation of the world-famous Bohemian glass (also called Bohemian Crystal). In pre-Hussite times they produced amazing works of vitreous art near Daubitz, nowadays called Doubice.

1. In traditional societies, _____ are two central components of religious practice. Although _____ are commonly united as parts of religion, the exact relationship between them has been a matter of controversy among scholars. One of the approaches to this problem is 'the _____, or myth-ritualist, theory', which holds that 'myth does not stand by itself but is tied to ritual'.

   a. Bagar
   b. Prague school
   c. Myth and ritual
   d. Moshe Safdie

2. . _____ is a school of Hellenistic philosophy founded in Athens by Zeno of Citium in the early 3rd century BC.

The Stoics taught that destructive emotions resulted from errors in judgment, and that a sage, or person of 'moral and intellectual perfection,' would not suffer such emotions.

Stoics were concerned with the active relationship between cosmic determinism and human freedom, and the belief that it is virtuous to maintain a will (called prohairesis) that is in accord with nature.

a. Strength Through Peace
b. Substitutionism
c. Stoicism
d. Supremacism

3. _____ is a UK funded research project seeking do build capacity in generic modelling tools and simulation techniques for complex systems. Its acronym stands for Complex Systems Modelling and Simulation. This is a four-year project, running from 2007 to 2011 as a collaboration between the University of York and Kent, with further collaborations from the University of Abertay Dundee and Bristol Robotics Laboratory.

a. Darwin among the Machines
b. CoSMoS
c. Holism
d. Hyle

4. _____ is any scientific theory concerning the coming into existence, or origin, of the cosmos or universe, or about how what sentient beings perceive as 'reality' came to be. The word comes from the Greek κοσμογον?α or κοσμογεν?α and the root of γ?(γ)νομαι / γ?γονα . In astronomy, _____ refers to the study of the origin of particular astrophysical objects or systems, and is most commonly used in reference to the origin of the solar system.

a. De mirabilibus sacrae scripturae
b. De rerum natura
c. Cosmogony
d. Hyle

5. Dame _____ DBE (15 July 1919 - 8 February 1999) was an Irish-born British author and philosopher, best known for her novels about political and social questions of good and evil, sexual relationships, morality, and the power of the unconscious. Her first published novel, Under the Net, was selected in 1998 as one of Modern Library's 100 best English-language novels of the 20th century. In 1987, she was made a Dame Commander of the Order of the British Empire.

a. Alan Musgrave
b. Richard Lewis Nettleship
c. Iris Murdoch
d. William Nicholson

1. c
2. c
3. b
4. c
5. c

You can take the complete Chapter Practice Test

for 4. The Creative Functions of Myth and Ritual: Performing the World
on all key terms, persons, places, and concepts.

Online 99 Cents

http://www.JustTheFacts101.com

Use www.JustTheFacts101.com for all your study needs

including Facts101's online interactive problem solving labs in

chemistry, statistics, mathematics, and more.

5. Religion, Nature, and Science: The Super Natural

_____ | John William Draper _____

_____ | Merton Thesis _____

_____ | Mysticism _____

_____ | Philosophical analysis _____

_____ | Cosmogony _____

_____ | Protestantism _____

_____ | Atheism _____

_____ | Ecology _____

_____ | Thunder god _____

_____ | Purity _____

_____ | Caste _____

_____ | Torah _____

_____ | Structuralism _____

_____ | Soul _____

_____ | Cosmology _____

_____ | Paranormal _____

_____ | Religious experience _____

_____ | Deep ecology _____

_____ | Nature religion _____

_____ | Charles Robert Darwin _____

_____ | Spinoza _____

5. Religion, Nature, and Science: The Super Natural

CHAPTER OUTLINE: KEY TERMS, PEOPLE, PLACES, CONCEPTS

Animism

Environmentalism

Monotheism

Panpsychism

Spirituality

Darwinism

Thomas Nagel

Anthropocentrism

Liberation theology

Materialism

Skepticism

Theology

Friedrich

CoSMoS

Telepathy

Shamanism

Axial Age

Avatar

Terence McKenna

5. Religion, Nature, and Science: The Super Natural

John William Draper	John William Draper was an American scientist, philosopher, physician, chemist, historian, and photographer. Early life John William Draper was born May 5, 1811 in St. Helens, Merseyside, England to John Christopher Draper, a Wesleyan clergyman and Sarah (Ripley) Draper. He also had three sisters, Dorothy Catherine, Elizabeth Johnson, and Sarah Ripley.
Merton Thesis	The Merton Thesis is an argument about the nature of early experimental science proposed by Robert K. Merton. Similar to Max Weber's famous claim on the link between Protestant ethic and the capitalist economy, Merton argued for a similar positive correlation between the rise of Protestant pietism and early experimental science. The Merton Thesis has resulted in continuous debates.
Mysticism	Mysticism is the pursuit of communion with, identity with divinity, spiritual truth intuition, instinct or insight. Mysticism usually centers on a practice or practices intended to nurture those experiences or awareness. Mysticism may be dualistic, maintaining a distinction between the self and the divine, or may be nondualistic.
Philosophical analysis	Philosophical analysis is a general term for techniques typically used by philosophers in the analytic tradition that involve 'breaking down' (i.e. analyzing) philosophical issues.
Cosmogony	Cosmogony is any scientific theory concerning the coming into existence, or origin, of the cosmos or universe, or about how what sentient beings perceive as 'reality' came to be. The word comes from the Greek κοσμογον?α or κοσμογεν?α and the root of γ?(γ)νομαι / γ?γονα . In astronomy, cosmogony refers to the study of the origin of particular astrophysical objects or systems, and is most commonly used in reference to the origin of the solar system.
Protestantism	Protestantism is a branch within Christianity, containing many denominations of different practices and doctrines, that originated in the sixteenth-century Protestant Reformation. It is considered to be one of the primary divisions within the original Christian church, i.e., the Catholic Church, along with Eastern Orthodoxy. Some groups that are often loosely labeled 'Protestant' do not use the term to define themselves, and some tend to reject it because of the implication of being non-traditional.
Atheism	Atheism is, in a broad sense, the rejection of belief in the existence of deities. In a narrower sense, atheism is specifically the position that there are no deities. Most inclusively, atheism is simply the absence of belief that any deities exist.
Ecology	Ecology is the scientific study of the relations that living organisms have with respect to each other and their natural environment.

	Variables of interest to ecologists include the composition, distribution, amount (biomass), number, and changing states of organisms within and among ecosystems. Ecosystems are hierarchical systems that are organized into a graded series of regularly interacting and semi-independent parts (e.g., species) that aggregate into higher orders of complex integrated wholes (e.g., communities).
Thunder god	Polytheistic peoples of many cultures have postulated a Thunder god, the personification or source of the forces of thunder and lightning. Frequently, the Thunder god is known as the chief or king of the gods, for example Zeus in Greek mythology, or Indra in Hindu mythology, or otherwise a close relation, for example Thor, son of Odin, in Norse mythology.

· Teshub · Adad, Ishkur, Marduk (Babylonian-Assyrian mythology) · Hadad (Levantine mythology)

· Tarhunt (Hittite/Luwian mythology) · Zeus · Brontes · Jupiter, Summanus (Roman mythology) · Taranis (Pan-Celtic); Ambisagrus, Leucetios, (Gaulish mythology) · Þunraz · Thor · Perkunos (Balto-Slavic; Lithuanian Perkunas, Slavic Per(k)un) · Perëndi (Albanian mythology) · Gebeleizis (Dacian mythology) · Zibelthiurdos (Thracian mythology) · Ukko or Perkele (Finnish mythology) · Horagalles (Sami mythology) · Aplu (Etruscan mythology)

· Lei Gong · Ajisukitakahikone, Raijin , Tenjin (kami) · Susanoo · Indra, Parjanya (Hindu mythology)

· Thunderbird (Native American mythology) · Xolotl (Aztec and Toltec mythology) · Chaac (Maya mythology) · Apocatequil (Incan mythology) · Cocijo (Mexican mythology) · Aktzin (Mexican mythology) · Jasso (Mexican mythology) · Haokah (Lakota mythology) · Tupã (Guaraní mythology, Brazil)

· Set (god) (Egyptian mythology) · Shango (Yorùbá mythology) · Oya (goddess of thunder, Yoruba mythology) · Azaka-Tonnerre (West African Vodun/Haitian Vodou) · Mulungu · Xevioso (alternately: Xewioso, Heviosso. |
| Purity | Purity (suddha) is an important concept within much of Theravada and Mahayana Buddhism, although the implications of the resultant moral purification may be viewed differently in the varying traditions. The aim is to purify the personality of the Buddhist practitioner so that all moral and character defilements and defects (kleshas such as anger, ignorance and lust) are wiped away and Nirvana can be obtained.

Theravada Buddhism regards the path of self-purification as absolutely vital for the reaching of nibbana/nirvana. |
| Caste | A caste is a combined social system of occupation, endogamy, culture, social class, and political power. caste should not be confused with class, in that members of a caste are deemed to be alike in function or culture, whereas not all members of a defined class may be so alike. |

5. Religion, Nature, and Science: The Super Natural

Torah	The term 'Torah' , refers either to the Five Books of Moses or to the entirety of Judaism's founding legal and ethical religious texts. A 'Sefer Torah' (×¡Öµ×¤Ö¶×¨¨ ×ªÖ¼×¾•Ö¹×¨Ö¸×", 'book of Torah') or Torah scroll, is a copy of the Torah written on parchment in a formal, traditional manner by a specially trained scribe under very strict requirements. The Torah is the first of three parts of the Tanakh , the founding religious document of Judaism, Messiannic, and Hebrew belief, and is divided into five books, whose names in English are Genesis, Exodus, Leviticus, Numbers, and Deuteronomy, in reference to their themes .
Structuralism	Structuralism is a theoretical paradigm that emphasizes that elements of culture must be understood in terms of their relationship to a larger, overarching system or 'structure.' Alternately, as summarized by philosopher Simon Blackburn, Structuralism is 'the belief that phenomena of human life are not intelligible except through their interrelations. These relations constitute a structure, and behind local variations in the surface phenomena there are constant laws of abstract culture'. Structuralism originated in the early 1900s, in the structural linguistics of Ferdinand de Saussure and the subsequent Prague, Moscow and Copenhagen schools of linguistics.
Soul	The soul--in many traditional spiritual, philosophical, and psychological traditions--is the incorporeal and immortal essence of a person, living thing, or object. According to some religions (including the Abrahamic religions in most of their forms), souls--or at least immortal souls capable of union with the divine--belong only to human beings. For example, the Catholic theologian Thomas Aquinas attributed 'soul' (anima) to all organisms but taught that only human souls are immortal.
Cosmology	Cosmology is the academic discipline that seeks to understand the origin, evolution, structure, and ultimate fate of the Universe at large, as well as the natural laws that keep it in order. Modern cosmology is dominated by the Big Bang theory, which brings together observational astronomy and particle physics. Although the word cosmology is recent (first used in 1730 in Christian Wolff's Cosmologia Generalis), the study of the universe has a long history involving science, philosophy, esotericism and religion.
Paranormal	Paranormal is a general term that describes unusual experiences that supposedly lack a scientific explanation, or phenomena alleged to be outside of science's current ability to explain or measure. Notably, Paranormal phenomena also lack scientific evidence, as detectable but not well explained phenomena such as dark matter or dark energy are not commonly called Paranormal. In parapsychology, the term has, in the past, been used to describe the supposed phenomena of extra-sensory perception, including telepathy, and psychokinesis, ghosts, and hauntings.

Religious experience	A religious experience is a subjective experience in which an individual reports contact with a transcendent reality, an encounter or union with the divine. Such an experience often involves arriving at some knowledge or insight previously unavailable to the subject yet unaccountable or unforseeable according to the usual conceptual or psychological framework within which the subject has been used to operating. Religious experience generally brings understanding, partial or complete, of issues of a fundamental character that may have been a cause (whether consciously ackowledged or not) of anguish or alienation to the subject for an extended period of time.
Deep ecology	Deep ecology is a contemporary ecological philosophy that recognizes an inherent worth of all living beings, regardless of their instrumental utility to human needs. The philosophy emphasizes the interdependence of organisms within ecosystems and that of ecosystems with each other within the biosphere. It provides a foundation for the environmental, ecology and green movements and has fostered a new system of environmental ethics.
Nature religion	Nature religion is an academic term used to refer to those religious movements which believe that the natural world is an embodiment of divinity, sacredness or spiritual power. It does not denote any particular religious movement per se, instead being used in reference to a variety of different religious groups and sub-groups. Various different religious movements are often included under the umbrella definition of 'nature religion'.
Charles Robert Darwin	Charles Robert Darwin FRS (12 February 1809 - 19 April 1882) was an English naturalist who established that all species of life have descended over time from common ancestors, and proposed the scientific theory that this branching pattern of evolution resulted from a process that he called natural selection. He published his theory with compelling evidence for evolution in his 1859 book On the Origin of Species. The scientific community and much of the general public came to accept evolution as a fact in his lifetime, but it was not until the emergence of the modern evolutionary synthesis from the 1930s to the 1950s that a broad consensus developed that natural selection was the basic mechanism of evolution.
Spinoza	Baruch or Benedict de Spinoza was a Dutch philosopher of Portuguese Jewish origin. Revealing considerable scientific aptitude, the breadth and importance of Spinoza's work was not fully realized until years after his death. Today, he is considered one of the great rationalists of 17th-century philosophy, laying the groundwork for the 18th century Enlightenment and modern biblical criticism.
Animism	Animism is a philosophical, religious or spiritual idea that souls or spirits exist not only in humans but also in other animals, plants, rocks, natural phenomena such as thunder, geographic features such as mountains or rivers a proposition also known as hylozoism in philosophy. Animism may further attribute souls to abstract concepts such as words, true names or metaphors in mythology.

5. Religion, Nature, and Science: The Super Natural

Environmentalism	Environmentalism is a broad philosophy, ideology and social movement regarding concerns for environmental conservation and improvement of the health of the environment, particularly as the measure for this health seeks to incorporate the concerns of non-human elements. Environmentalism advocates the preservation, restoration and/or improvement of the natural environment, and may be referred to as a movement to control pollution. For this reason, concepts such as a Land Ethic, Environmental Ethics, Biodiversity, Ecology and the Biophilia hypothesis figure predominantly.
Monotheism	Monotheism is the belief in the existence of one god, as distinguished from polytheism, the belief in more than one god, and atheism, the absence of belief in any god or gods. Monotheism is characteristic of the Abrahamic religions, (Judaism, Christianity, Islam and Baha'i Faith), but is also present in Neoplatonism and in Sikhism and it is difficult to delineate from notions such as pantheism and monism. Ostensibly monotheistic religions may still include concepts of a plurality of the divine; for example, the Trinity, in which God is one being in three eternal persons (the Father, the Son and the Holy Spirit).
Panpsychism	In philosophy, panpsychism is the view that all matter has a mental aspect, or, alternatively, all objects have a unified center of experience or point of view. Baruch Spinoza, Gottfried Leibniz, Gustav Theodor Fechner, Friedrich Paulsen, Ernst Haeckel, Charles Strong, and partially William James are considered panpsychists. Panexperientialism, as espoused by Alfred North Whitehead, is a less bold variation, which credits all entities with phenomenal consciousness but not with cognition, and therefore not necessarily with full-fledged minds.
Spirituality	Spirituality refers to an ultimate or an alleged immaterial reality; an inner path enabling a person to discover the essence of his/her being; or the 'deepest values and meanings by which people live.' Spiritual practices, including meditation, prayer and contemplation, are intended to develop an individual's inner life; spiritual experience includes that of connectedness with a larger reality, yielding a more comprehensive self; with other individuals or the human community; with nature or the cosmos; or with the divine realm. Spirituality is often experienced as a source of inspiration or orientation in life. It can encompass belief in immaterial realities or experiences of the immanent or transcendent nature of the world.
Darwinism	Darwinism is a set of movements and concepts related to ideas of transmutation of species or evolution, including ideas with no connection to the work of Charles Darwin. The meaning of 'Darwinism' has changed over time, and varies depending on who is using the term.

5. Religion, Nature, and Science: The Super Natural

Thomas Nagel	Thomas Nagel is an American philosopher, currently University Professor of Philosophy and Law at New York University, where he has taught since 1980. His main areas of philosophical interest are philosophy of mind, political philosophy and ethics. He is well known for his critique of reductionist accounts of the mind in his essay 'What Is It Like to Be a Bat?' (1974), and for his contributions to deontological and liberal moral and political theory in The Possibility of Altruism (1970) and subsequent writings. Nagel was born July 4, 1937, in Belgrade, Yugoslavia (now Serbia) to a Jewish family.
Anthropocentrism	Anthropocentrism describes an analysis from the perspective that human beings are the central, only or most significant animal species, or the assessment of reality through an exclusively human perspective. The term can be used interchangeably with humanocentrism, while the first concept can also be referred to as human supremacy. Anthropocentrism is a major concept in the field of environmental ethics and environmental philosophy, where it is often considered to be the root cause of problems created by human interaction with the environment, however; it is profoundly embedded in our culture and conscious acts.
Liberation theology	Liberation theology is a political movement in Christian theology which interprets the teachings of Jesus Christ in terms of a liberation from unjust economic, political, or social conditions. It has been described by proponents as 'an interpretation of Christian faith through the poor's suffering, their struggle and hope, and a critique of society and the Catholic faith and Christianity through the eyes of the poor', and by detractors as Christianized Marxism. Although liberation theology has grown into an international and inter-denominational movement, it began as a movement within the Roman Catholic church in Latin America in the 1950s-1960s.
Materialism	In philosophy, the theory of materialism holds that the only thing that exists is matter or energy; that all things are composed of material and all phenomena (including consciousness) are the result of material interactions. In other words, matter is the only substance, and reality is identical with the actually occurring states of energy and matter. To many philosophers, 'materialism' is synonymous with 'physicalism'.
Skepticism	Skepticism, but generally refers to any questioning attitude towards knowledge, facts, or opinions/beliefs stated as facts, or doubt regarding claims that are taken for granted elsewhere. The word may characterize a position on a single matter, as in the case of religious skepticism, which is 'doubt concerning basic religious principles (such as immortality, providence, and revelation)', but philosophical skepticism is an overall approach that requires all information to be well supported by evidence. Skeptics may even doubt the reliability of their own senses.

5. Religion, Nature, and Science: The Super Natural

Theology	Theology is the rational and systematic study of religion and its influences and of the nature of religious truth, or the learned profession acquired by specialized courses in religion, usually taught at a college or seminary. Augustine of Hippo defined the Latin equivalent, theologia, as 'reasoning or discussion concerning the Deity'; Richard Hooker defined 'theology' in English as 'the science of things divine'. The term can, however, be used for a variety of different disciplines or forms of discourse.
Friedrich	The Friedrich are the most ancient German-Bohemian glass-maker family. History From as early as 750 years ago, the shadowy picture of the oldest German-Bohemian glass-maker family Friedrich emerges, who contributed greatly towards the creation of the world-famous Bohemian glass (also called Bohemian Crystal). In pre-Hussite times they produced amazing works of vitreous art near Daubitz, nowadays called Doubice.
CoSMoS	CoSMoS is a UK funded research project seeking do build capacity in generic modelling tools and simulation techniques for complex systems. Its acronym stands for Complex Systems Modelling and Simulation. This is a four-year project, running from 2007 to 2011 as a collaboration between the University of York and Kent, with further collaborations from the University of Abertay Dundee and Bristol Robotics Laboratory.
Telepathy	Telepathy , is the ostensible transfer of information on thoughts or feelings between individuals by means other than the five senses. The term was coined in 1882 by the classical scholar Fredric W. H. Myers, a founder of the Society for Psychical Research, specifically to replace the earlier expression thought-transference.
Shamanism	Shamanism is a term used in a variety of anthropological, historical and popular contexts to refer to certain magico-religious practices that involve a practitioner reaching altered states of consciousness in order to encounter and interact with the spirit world. A shaman is a person regarded as having access to, and influence in, the world of benevolent and malevolent spirits, who typically enters a trance state during a ritual, and practices divination and healing. The exact definition and use of the term 'shamanism' has been highly debated by scholars, with no clear consensus on the issue.
Axial Age	Axial Age or Axial Period (Ger. Achsenzeit, 'axis time') is a term coined by German philosopher Karl Jaspers to describe the period from 800 to 200 BC, during which, according to Jaspers, similar revolutionary thinking appeared in India, China and the Occident. The period is also sometimes referred to as the Axis Age.

Avatar	In Hinduism, avatar, or a descent of the Supreme Being (i.e., Vishnu for Vaishnavites) and is mostly translated into English as 'incarnation', but more accurately as 'appearance' or 'manifestation'. The term is most often associated with Vishnu, though it has also come to be associated with other deities. Varying lists of avatars of Vishnu appear in Hindu scriptures, including the ten Dashavatara of the Garuda Purana and the twenty-two avatars in the Bhagavata Purana, though the latter adds that the incarnations of Vishnu are innumerable.
Terence McKenna	Terence Kemp McKenna (November 16, 1946 - April 3, 2000) was an American philosopher, psychonaut, researcher, teacher, lecturer and writer on many subjects, such as human consciousness, language, psychedelic drugs, the evolution of civilizations, the origin and end of the universe, alchemy, and extraterrestrial beings. Early life Terence McKenna grew up in Paonia, Colorado. He was introduced to geology through his uncle and developed a hobby of solitary fossil hunting in the arroyos near his home.

1. _____ describes an analysis from the perspective that human beings are the central, only or most significant animal species, or the assessment of reality through an exclusively human perspective.

The term can be used interchangeably with humanocentrism, while the first concept can also be referred to as human supremacy. _____ is a major concept in the field of environmental ethics and environmental philosophy, where it is often considered to be the root cause of problems created by human interaction with the environment, however; it is profoundly embedded in our culture and conscious acts.

   a. Emergent evolution
   b. Anthropocentrism
   c. Exclusivism
   d. Extropianism

2. . _____ is the rational and systematic study of religion and its influences and of the nature of religious truth, or the learned profession acquired by specialized courses in religion, usually taught at a college or seminary.

Augustine of Hippo defined the Latin equivalent, theologia, as 'reasoning or discussion concerning the Deity'; Richard Hooker defined '_____' in English as 'the science of things divine'. The term can, however, be used for a variety of different disciplines or forms of discourse.

a. Denis Alexander
b. Dawkins' God: Genes, Memes, and the Meaning of Life
c. Dwight H. Terry Lectureship
d. Theology

3. The _____ is an argument about the nature of early experimental science proposed by Robert K. Merton. Similar to Max Weber's famous claim on the link between Protestant ethic and the capitalist economy, Merton argued for a similar positive correlation between the rise of Protestant pietism and early experimental science. The _____ has resulted in continuous debates.

a. New social movements
b. Parallel Polis
c. Merton Thesis
d. Davis-Moore hypothesis

4. The _____--in many traditional spiritual, philosophical, and psychological traditions--is the incorporeal and immortal essence of a person, living thing, or object. According to some religions (including the Abrahamic religions in most of their forms), _____s--or at least immortal _____s capable of union with the divine--belong only to human beings. For example, the Catholic theologian Thomas Aquinas attributed '_____' (anima) to all organisms but taught that only human _____s are immortal.

a. Transhumanism
b. Turritopsis nutricula
c. Soul
d. Symbol theory

5. _____ is any scientific theory concerning the coming into existence, or origin, of the cosmos or universe, or about how what sentient beings perceive as 'reality' came to be. The word comes from the Greek κοσμογον?α or κοσμογεν? α and the root of γ?(γ)νομαι / γ?γονα . In astronomy, _____ refers to the study of the origin of particular astrophysical objects or systems, and is most commonly used in reference to the origin of the solar system.

a. De mirabilibus sacrae scripturae
b. Cosmogony
c. Holism
d. Hyle

1. b
2. d
3. c
4. c
5. b

You can take the complete Chapter Practice Test

for 5. Religion, Nature, and Science: The Super Natural
on all key terms, persons, places, and concepts.

Online 99 Cents

http://www.JustTheFacts101.com

Use www.JustTheFacts101.com for all your study needs

including Facts101's online interactive problem solving labs in

chemistry, statistics, mathematics, and more.

6. Sex and the Bodies of Religion: Seed and Soil

CHAPTER OUTLINE: KEY TERMS, PEOPLE, PLACES, CONCEPTS

	Adam and Eve
	Purity
	Metaphor
	Monotheism
	Ecstasy
	Myth and ritual
	Creation myth
	Feminist criticism
	Sexual orientation
	Quran
	Asceticism
	Celibacy
	Jainism
	Expression
	Patriarchy
	Piety
	Relativism
	Violence
	Inheritance
	Cicero
	Digambar

6. Sex and the Bodies of Religion: Seed and Soil

	Nostra Aetate
	Buddhism
	Hermes Trismegistus
	I Ching
	Iconoclasm
	Tantra
	Yoga
	Gospel
	Quakers
	Renaissance
	Society
	Attitude
	Mysticism
	Philosophical analysis
	Divinity
	Humanities
	Transcendence
	Kabbalah
	Plato
	Cosmogony
	Cosmology

6. Sex and the Bodies of Religion: Seed and Soil

CHAPTER OUTLINE: KEY TERMS, PEOPLE, PLACES, CONCEPTS

	EPIC
	Equality
	Critical theory
	Criticism
	Historical criticism
	Shaker
	Spinoza
	Dissociation
	Psychoanalysis
	Reflexivity
	Sexual abuse
	Charisma
	CoSMoS
	Panentheism
	Religious experience
	Election
	Theology
	Oracle
	Miracles
	Social change
	Theory

	Oedipus complex
	Institution
	Jerusalem
	Torah
	Religious law
	Sharia
	Canon law
	Confucianism
	Last Judgment
	Ernst Bergmann
	Belief
	Perspective
	Sociology
	Protestantism
	Sect
	John Calvin
	Meister Eckhart
	Gopnik
	Spiritual But Not Religious
	Agnosticism
	Materialism

	Paranormal
	Representation
	Skepticism
	Spiritualism
	Charles Robert Darwin

CHAPTER HIGHLIGHTS & NOTES: KEY TERMS, PEOPLE, PLACES, CONCEPTS

| Adam and Eve | Adam and Eve were, according to the Book of Genesis, the first man and woman created by YHWH . In theology and in folklore studies, the technical term 'protoplasts' is sometimes used for the first humans in this sense.

Narrative

Genesis 2

Genesis 2 opens with God fashioning a man from the dust and blowing life into his nostrils. |
|---|---|
| Purity | Purity (suddha) is an important concept within much of Theravada and Mahayana Buddhism, although the implications of the resultant moral purification may be viewed differently in the varying traditions. The aim is to purify the personality of the Buddhist practitioner so that all moral and character defilements and defects (kleshas such as anger, ignorance and lust) are wiped away and Nirvana can be obtained.

Theravada Buddhism regards the path of self-purification as absolutely vital for the reaching of nibbana/nirvana. |
| Metaphor | A metaphor is a literary figure of speech that describes a subject by asserting that it is, on some point of comparison, the same as another otherwise unrelated object. Metaphor is a type of analogy and is closely related to other rhetorical figures of speech that achieve their effects via association, comparison or resemblance including allegory, hyperbole, and simile. |

6. Sex and the Bodies of Religion: Seed and Soil

	One of the most prominent examples of a metaphor in English literature is the All the world's a stage monologue from As You Like It:All the world's a stage,And all the men and women merely players;They have their exits and their entrances; -- William Shakespeare, As You Like It, 2/7 This quote is a metaphor because the world is not literally a stage.
Monotheism	Monotheism is the belief in the existence of one god, as distinguished from polytheism, the belief in more than one god, and atheism, the absence of belief in any god or gods. Monotheism is characteristic of the Abrahamic religions, (Judaism, Christianity, Islam and Baha'i Faith), but is also present in Neoplatonism and in Sikhism and it is difficult to delineate from notions such as pantheism and monism. Ostensibly monotheistic religions may still include concepts of a plurality of the divine; for example, the Trinity, in which God is one being in three eternal persons (the Father, the Son and the Holy Spirit).
Ecstasy	Ecstasy from the Ancient Greek, ?κ-στασις (ek-stasis), is a subjective experience of total involvement of the subject, with an object of his or her awareness. Total involvement with an object of interest is not an ordinary experience because of being aware of other objects, thus ecstasy is an example of an altered state of consciousness characterized by diminished awareness of other objects or the total lack of the awareness of surroundings and everything around the object. For instance, if one is concentrating on a physical task, then one might cease to be aware of any intellectual thoughts.
Myth and ritual	In traditional societies, Myth and ritual are two central components of religious practice. Although Myth and ritual are commonly united as parts of religion, the exact relationship between them has been a matter of controversy among scholars. One of the approaches to this problem is 'the Myth and ritual, or myth-ritualist, theory', which holds that 'myth does not stand by itself but is tied to ritual'.
Creation myth	A creation myth is a symbolic narrative of a culture, tradition or people that describes their earliest beginnings, how the world they know began and how they first came into it. Creation myths develop in oral traditions, and are the most common form of myth, found throughout human culture. In the society in which it is told, a creation myth is usually regarded as conveying profound truths, although not necessarily in a historical or literal sense.
Feminist criticism	Feminist criticism is a type of literary criticism, which was developed in the late 1960s, focusing on the role of women in literature. Two important representatives are Virginia Woolf and Simone de Beauvoir who claim that women are a subject and no object.

Sexual orientation	Sexual orientation is a social construct used to describe a pattern of emotional, romantic, and/or sexual attractions to men, women, both genders, neither gender, or another gender. According to the American Psychological Association Sexual orientation also refers to a person's sense of 'personal and social identity based on those attractions, behaviors expressing them, and membership in a community of others who share them.' Sexual orientation is usually classified relative to the gender of the people who are found sexually attractive. Though people may use other labels, or none at all, Sexual orientation is usually discussed in terms of three categories: heterosexual, homosexual, and bisexual.
Quran	The Quran, also transliterated Qur'an, Koran, Al-Coran, Coran, Kuran, and Al-Qur'an, is the central religious text of Islam, which Muslims consider the verbatim word of God . It is regarded widely as the finest piece of literature in the Arabic language. The Quran is composed of verses (Ayah) that make up 114 chapters (suras) of unequal length which are classified either as Meccan or Medinan depending upon the place and time of their claimed revelation.
Asceticism	Asceticism describes a lifestyle characterized by abstinence from various worldly pleasures, often with the aim of pursuing religious and spiritual goals. Many religious traditions (e.g. Buddhism, Jainism, the Christian desert fathers) include practices that involve restraint with respect to actions of body, speech, and mind. The founders and earliest practitioners of these religions lived extremely austere lifestyles, refraining from sensual pleasures and the accumulation of material wealth.
Celibacy	Celibacy refers to a state of being unmarried, or a state of abstinence from sexual intercourse or the abstention by vow from marriage. The English word celibacy derives from the Latin caelibatus, 'state of being unmarried', from Latin caelebs, meaning 'unmarried'. This word derives from two Proto-Indo-European stems, *kaiwelo- 'alone' and *lib(h)s- 'living'.
Jainism	Jainism, is an Indian religion that prescribes a path of non-violence towards all living beings. Its philosophy and practice emphasize the necessity of self-effort to move the soul towards divine consciousness and liberation. Any soul that has conquered its own inner enemies and achieved the state of supreme being is called a jina ('conqueror' or 'victor').
Expression	In mathematics, an expression is a finite combination of symbols that is well-formed according to rules that depend on the context. Symbols can designate numbers (constants), variables, operations, functions, and other mathematical symbols, as well as punctuation, symbols of grouping, and other syntactic symbols. The use of expressions can range from the simple: $0 + 0$

6. Sex and the Bodies of Religion: Seed and Soil

to the complex: $$f(a) + \sum_{k=1}^{n} \frac{1}{k!} \frac{d^k}{dt^k} \bigg|_{t=0} f(u(t)) + \int_0^1 \frac{(1-t)^n}{n!} \frac{d^{n+1}}{dt^{n+1}} f(u(t)) \, dt.$$

We can think of algebraic expressions as generalizations of common arithmetic operations that are formed by combining numbers, variables, and mathematical operations.

Patriarchy

Patriarchy is a social system in which the role of the male as the primary authority figure is central to social organization, and where fathers hold authority over women, children, and property. It implies the institutions of male rule and privilege, and is dependent on female subordination.

Historically, the principle of patriarchy has been central to the social, legal, political, and economic organization of Celtic, Germanic, Roman, Greek, Hebrew, Arabian, Indian, and Chinese cultures, and has had a deep influence on modern civilization.

Piety

In spiritual terminology, piety is a virtue that can mean religious devotion, spirituality, or a combination of both. A common element in most conceptions of piety is humility.

The word piety comes from the Latin word pietas, the noun form of the adjective pius (which means 'devout' or 'good').

Relativism

Relativism is the concept that points of view have no absolute truth or validity, having only relative, subjective value according to differences in perception and consideration. The term is often used to refer to the context of moral principle, where in a relativistic mode of thought, principles and ethics are regarded as applicable in only limited context. There are many forms of relativism which vary in their degree of controversy.

Violence

Violence is defined by the World Health Organization as the intentional use of physical force or power, threatened or actual, against oneself, another person, or against a group or community, that either results in or has a high likelihood of resulting in injury, death, psychological harm, maldevelopment or deprivation. This definition associates intentionality with the committing of the act itself, irrespective of the outcome it produces.

Globally, violence takes the lives of more than 1.5 million people annually: just over 50% due to suicide, some 35% due to homicide, and just over 12% as a direct result of war or some other form of conflict.

Inheritance

Inheritance is the practice of passing on property, titles, debts, and obligations upon the death of an individual. It has long played an important role in human societies. The rules of inheritance differ between societies and have changed over time.

Cicero	Marcus Tullius Cicero was a Roman philosopher, statesman, lawyer, orator, political theorist, Roman consul and constitutionalist. He came from a wealthy municipal family of the equestrian order, and is widely considered one of Rome's greatest orators and prose stylists. He introduced the Romans to the chief schools of Greek philosophy and created a Latin philosophical vocabulary (with neologisms such as humanitas, qualitas, quantitas, and essentia) distinguishing himself as a linguist, translator, and philosopher.
Digambar	Digambar , has many different meaning and associations throughout Dharmic traditions. Many representations of deities within these traditions are depicted as sky-clad, eg. Samantabhadra/Samantabhadri in yab-yum.
Nostra Aetate	Nostra Aetate is the Declaration on the Relation of the Church with Non-Christian Religions of the Second Vatican Council. Passed by a vote of 2,221 to 88 of the assembled bishops, this declaration was promulgated on October 28, 1965, by Pope Paul VI. The first draft, entitled 'Decree on the Jews' , was completed in November 1961, approximately fourteen months after Cardinal Bea was commissioned by Pope John XXIII. This draft essentially went nowhere, never having been submitted to the Council, which opened on 11 October 1962. · Introduction · Hindus, Buddhists, and other religions · Muslims · Jews · Conclusion · The Declaration begins by describing the unity of the origin of all people, and the fact that they all return to God; hence their final goal is also one.
Buddhism	Buddhism is a religion and philosophy indigenous to the Indian subcontinent that encompasses a variety of traditions, beliefs, and practices largely based on teachings attributed to Siddhartha Gautama, who is commonly known as the Buddha . The Buddha lived and taught in the eastern part of Indian subcontinent some time between the 6th and 4th centuries BCE. He is recognized by Buddhists as an awakened or enlightened teacher who shared his insights to help sentient beings end suffering (dukkha) through eliminating ignorance (avidya), craving , and hatred, by way of understanding and seeing dependent origination (pratityasamutpada) and non-self (anatman), and thus attain the highest happiness, nirvana (nirvana). Two major branches of Buddhism are recognized: Theravada ('The School of the Elders') and Mahayana ('The Great Vehicle').
Hermes Trismegistus	MythologyHermes Trismegistus Â· Thoth Â· Poimandres HermeticaCorpus Hermeticum Â· Kybalion Three Parts of the Wisdom of the Whole UniverseAlchemy Â· Astrology Â· Theurgy

	Influence and Influences
	Hermetic MovementsRosicrucianism
	OrdersHermetic Order of the Golden Dawn Â· Hermetic Brotherhood of Luxor Â· Hermetic Brotherhood of Light
	Topics in HermetismQabalah Occult and divinatory tarot Hermetists and HermeticistsJohn Dee . Aleister Crowley Â· Israel RegardieThÄbit ibn Qurra Â· ParacelsusGiordano Bruno Â· Manly P. Hall Â· Samuel MacGregor Mathers Â· William WestcottFranz BardonHermes Trismegistus is the representation of the combination of the Greek god Hermes and the Egyptian god Thoth. In Hellenistic Egypt, the Greeks recognised the congruence of their God Hermes with the Egyptian god Thoth.
I Ching	The I Ching or 'Yì Jing' (pinyin), also known as the Classic of Changes, Book of Changes and Zhouyi, is one of the oldest of the Chinese classic texts. The book contains a divination system comparable to Western geomancy or the West African Ifá system; in Western cultures and modern East Asia, it is still widely used for this purpose.
	Traditionally, the I Ching and its hexagrams were thought to pre-date recorded history, and based on traditional Chinese accounts, its origins trace back to the 3rd to the 2nd millennium BC. Modern scholarship suggests that the earliest layer of the text may date from the end of the 2nd millennium BC, but place doubts on the mythological aspects in the traditional accounts.
Iconoclasm	Iconoclasm is the deliberate destruction of religious icons and other symbols or monuments, usually with religious or political motives. It is a frequent component of major political or religious changes. The term encompasses the more specific destruction of images of a ruler after his death or overthrow (damnatio memoriae), for example, following Akhenaten's death in Ancient Egypt.
Tantra	Tantra and the universe is regarded as the divine play of Shakti and Shiva. The word Tantra also applies to any of the scriptures (called 'Tantras') commonly identified with the worship of Shakti. Tantra deals primarily with spiritual practices and ritual forms of worship, which aim at liberation from ignorance and rebirth.
Yoga	Yoga refers to traditional physical and mental disciplines that originated in India. The word is associated with meditative practices in Hinduism, Buddhism and Jainism. Within Hinduism, it refers to one of the six orthodox (astika) schools of Hindu philosophy, and to the goal towards which that school directs its practices.
Gospel	A Gospel is a writing that describes the life of Jesus.

	The word is primarily used to refer to the four canonical Gospels: the Gospel of Matthew, Gospel of Mark, Gospel of Luke and Gospel of John, probably written between AD 65 and 80. They appear to have been originally untitled; they were quoted anonymously in the first half of the second century (i.e. 100-150) but the names by which they are currently known appear suddenly around the year 180. The first canonical Gospel written is thought by most scholars to be Mark (c 65-70), which was according to the majority used as a source for the Gospels of Matthew and Luke.
Quakers	Quakers, are members of the Religious Society of Friends, or Friends' Church--an international family of diverse Christian religious organizations that focus on the priesthood of all believers. Quakers today are theologically diverse: mostly regarded as Christian, they include those with evangelical, holiness, liberal and traditional Quaker understandings of Christianity. From the end of the 20th century, small but vocal groups of Friends with Christian atheist or universalist beliefs have emerged.
Renaissance	The Renaissance was a cultural movement that spanned the period roughly from the 14th to the 17th century, beginning in Italy in the Late Middle Ages and later spreading to the rest of Europe. Though the invention of printing sped the dissemination of ideas from the later 15th century, the changes of the Renaissance were not uniformly experienced across Europe. As a cultural movement, it encompassed innovative flowering of Latin and vernacular literatures, beginning with the 14th-century resurgence of learning based on classical sources, which contemporaries credited to Petrarch, the development of linear perspective and other techniques of rendering a more natural reality in painting, and gradual but widespread educational reform.
Society	A society, or a human society, is a group of people involved with each other through persistent relations, or a large social grouping sharing the same geographical or social territory, subject to the same political authority and dominant cultural expectations. Human societies are characterized by patterns of relationships (social relations) between individuals who share a distinctive culture and institutions; a given society may be described as the sum total of such relationships among its constituent members. In the social sciences, a larger society often evinces stratification and/or dominance patterns in subgroups.
Attitude	Attitude as a term of fine art refers to the posture or gesture given to a figure by a painter or sculptor. It applies to the body and not to a mental state, but the arrangement of the body is presumed to serve a communicative or expressive purpose. An example of a conventional attitude in art is proskynesis to indicate respect toward God, emperors, clerics of high status, and religious icons; in Byzantine art, it is particularly characteristic in depictions of the emperor paying homage to Christ.
Mysticism	Mysticism is the pursuit of communion with, identity with divinity, spiritual truth intuition, instinct or insight.

6. Sex and the Bodies of Religion: Seed and Soil

	Mysticism usually centers on a practice or practices intended to nurture those experiences or awareness. Mysticism may be dualistic, maintaining a distinction between the self and the divine, or may be nondualistic.
Philosophical analysis	Philosophical analysis is a general term for techniques typically used by philosophers in the analytic tradition that involve 'breaking down' (i.e. analyzing) philosophical issues.
Divinity	Divinity is the study of Christian and other theology and ministry at a school, divinity school, university, or seminary. The term is sometimes a synonym for theology as an academic, speculative pursuit, and sometimes is used for the study of applied theology and ministry to make a distinction between that and academic theology. It most often refers to Christian study which is linked with the professional degrees for ordained ministry or related work, though it is also used in an academic setting by other faith traditions.
Humanities	The humanities are academic disciplines that study the human condition, using methods that are primarily analytical, critical, or speculative, as distinguished from the mainly empirical approaches of the natural sciences.
	The humanities include ancient and modern languages, literature, history, philosophy, religion, and visual and performing arts such as music and theatre. The humanities that are also regarded as social sciences include technology, history, anthropology, area studies, communication studies, cultural studies, law and linguistics.
Transcendence	In religion, transcendence refers to the aspect of God's nature and power which is wholly independent of (and removed from) the material universe. This is contrasted with immanence where God is fully present in the physical world and thus accessible to creatures in various ways. In religious experience transcendence is a state of being that has overcome the limitations of physical existence and by some definitions has also become independent of it.
Kabbalah	Kabbalah, also spelled Kabala or Cabala, is an esoteric method, discipline and school of thought. Its definition varies according to the tradition and aims of those following it, from its religious origin as an integral part of Judaism, to Christian, New Age, or Occultist syncretic adaptions. Kabbalah is a set of esoteric teachings meant to explain the relationship between an unchanging, eternal and mysterious Ein Sof (no end) and the mortal and finite universe (his creation).
Plato	Plato was a Classical Greek philosopher, mathematician, student of Socrates, writer of philosophical dialogues, and founder of the Academy in Athens, the first institution of higher learning in the Western world. Along with his mentor, Socrates, and his student, Aristotle, Plato helped to lay the foundations of Western philosophy and science. In the words of A. N. Whitehead:'

Cosmogony	Cosmogony is any scientific theory concerning the coming into existence, or origin, of the cosmos or universe, or about how what sentient beings perceive as 'reality' came to be. The word comes from the Greek κοσμογον?α or κοσμογεν?α and the root of γ?(γ)νομαι / γ?γονα . In astronomy, cosmogony refers to the study of the origin of particular astrophysical objects or systems, and is most commonly used in reference to the origin of the solar system.
Cosmology	Cosmology is the academic discipline that seeks to understand the origin, evolution, structure, and ultimate fate of the Universe at large, as well as the natural laws that keep it in order. Modern cosmology is dominated by the Big Bang theory, which brings together observational astronomy and particle physics. Although the word cosmology is recent (first used in 1730 in Christian Wolff's Cosmologia Generalis), the study of the universe has a long history involving science, philosophy, esotericism and religion.
EPIC	EPIC (Executive-Process/Interactive Control) is a cognitive architecture developed by Professors David E. Kieras and David E. Meyer at the University of Michigan . EPIC has components that emulate various parts of the human-information processing system. Among these components are tools for perceptual, cognitive, and motor processing.
Equality	Loosely, equality is the state of being quantitatively the same. More formally, equality is the binary relation on a set X defined by $\{(x,x) \mid x \in X\}$. The identity relation is the archetype of the more general concept of an equivalence relation on a set: those binary relations which are reflexive, symmetric, and transitive. The relation of equality is also antisymmetric.
Critical theory	Critical theory is a school of thought that stresses the examination and critique of society and culture, drawing from knowledge across the social sciences and humanities. The term has two different meanings with different origins and histories: one originating in sociology and the other in literary criticism. This has led to the very literal use of 'critical theory' as an umbrella term to describe any theory founded upon critique.
Criticism	Criticism is the practice of judging the merits and faults of something or someone in an intelligible (or articulate) way. •The judger is called 'the critic'.•To engage in criticism is 'to criticize'.•One specific item of criticism is called 'a criticism'.

Criticism can be:•directed toward a person or an animal; at a group, authority or organization; at a specific behaviour; or at an object of some kind (an idea, a relationship, a condition, a process, or a thing).•personal (delivered directly from one person to another, in a personal capacity), or impersonal (expressing the view of an organization, and not aimed at anyone personally).•highly specific and detailed, or very abstract and general.•verbal (expressed in language) or non-verbal (expressed symbolically, or expressed through an action or a way of behaving).•explicit (the criticism is clearly stated) or implicit (a criticism is implied by what is being said, but it is not stated openly).•the result of critical thinking or spontaneous impulse.

To criticize does not necessarily imply 'to find fault', but the word is often taken to mean the simple expression of an objection against prejudice, or a disapproval. Often criticism involves active disagreement, but it may only mean 'taking sides'.

Historical criticism	
	Historical criticism, is a branch of literary criticism that investigates the origins of ancient text in order to understand 'the world behind the text'.

The primary goal of historical criticism is to ascertain the text's primitive or original meaning in its original historical context and its literal sense or sensus literalis historicus. The secondary goal seeks to establish a reconstruction of the historical situation of the author and recipients of the text. |
Shaker	A shaker is a device used in vibration testing to excite the structure either for endurance testing or modal testing. •Vibration.
Spinoza	Baruch or Benedict de Spinoza was a Dutch philosopher of Portuguese Jewish origin. Revealing considerable scientific aptitude, the breadth and importance of Spinoza's work was not fully realized until years after his death. Today, he is considered one of the great rationalists of 17th-century philosophy, laying the groundwork for the 18th century Enlightenment and modern biblical criticism.
Dissociation	Dissociation is an unexpected partial or complete disruption of the normal integration of a person's conscious or psychological functioning. Dissociation is a mental process that severs a connection to a person's thoughts, memories, feelings, actions, or sense of identity. Dissociation can be a response to trauma, and perhaps allows the mind to distance itself from experiences that are too much for the psyche to process at that time.
Psychoanalysis	Psychoanalysis is a body of ideas developed by Austrian neurologist Sigmund Freud and continued by others. It is primarily devoted to the study of human psychological functioning and behavior, although it can also be applied to societies.

	Psychoanalysis has three main components:•a method of investigation of the mind and the way one thinks;•a systematized set of theories about human behavior;•a method of treatment of psychological or emotional illness.
	Under the broad umbrella of psychoanalysis, there are at least 22 theoretical orientations regarding human mentation and development.
Reflexivity	Reflexivity refers to circular relationships between cause and effect. A reflexive relationship is bidirectional with both the cause and the effect affecting one another in a situation that does not render both functions causes and effects. In sociology, reflexivity therefore comes to mean an act of self-reference where examination or action 'bends back on', refers to, and affects the entity instigating the action or examination.
Sexual abuse	Sexual abuse, also referred to as molestation, is the forcing of undesired sexual behavior by one person upon another. When that force is immediate, of short duration, or infrequent, it is called sexual assault. The offender is referred to as a sexual abuser or (often pejoratively) molester.
Charisma	The term charisma has two senses: 1) compelling attractiveness or charm that can inspire devotion in others, 2) a divinely conferred power or talent. For some theological usages the term is rendered charism, with a meaning the same as sense 2.
CoSMoS	CoSMoS is a UK funded research project seeking do build capacity in generic modelling tools and simulation techniques for complex systems. Its acronym stands for Complex Systems Modelling and Simulation. This is a four-year project, running from 2007 to 2011 as a collaboration between the University of York and Kent, with further collaborations from the University of Abertay Dundee and Bristol Robotics Laboratory.
Panentheism	Panentheism (from Greek π?ν (pân) 'all'; ?ν (en) 'in'; and θε?ς (theós) 'God'; 'all-in-God') is a belief system which posits that the divine exists (be it a monotheistic God, polytheistic gods, or an eternal cosmic animating force), interpenetrates every part of nature and timelessly extends beyond it. Panentheism differentiates itself from pantheism, which holds that the divine is synonymous with the universe.
	In panentheism, the universe in the first formulation is practically the whole itself.
Religious experience	A religious experience is a subjective experience in which an individual reports contact with a transcendent reality, an encounter or union with the divine. Such an experience often involves arriving at some knowledge or insight previously unavailable to the subject yet unaccountable or unforeseeable according to the usual conceptual or psychological framework within which the subject has been used to operating.

6. Sex and the Bodies of Religion: Seed and Soil

Election	An election is a formal decision-making process by which a population chooses an individual to hold public office. Elections have been the usual mechanism by which modern representative democracy has operated since the 17th century. Elections may fill offices in the legislature, sometimes in the executive and judiciary, and for regional and local government.
Theology	Theology is the rational and systematic study of religion and its influences and of the nature of religious truth, or the learned profession acquired by specialized courses in religion, usually taught at a college or seminary. Augustine of Hippo defined the Latin equivalent, theologia, as 'reasoning or discussion concerning the Deity'; Richard Hooker defined 'theology' in English as 'the science of things divine'. The term can, however, be used for a variety of different disciplines or forms of discourse.
Oracle	An Oracle is a person or agency considered to be a source of wise counsel or prophetic opinion. It may also be a revealed prediction or precognition of the future, from deities, that is spoken through another object or life-form (e.g.: augury and auspice). In the ancient world many sites gained a reputation for the dispensing of oracular wisdom: they too became known as 'Oracles,' and the oracular utterances, called khrÄ"smoi in Greek, were often referred to under the same name--a name derived from the Latin verb ÅrÄre, to speak.
Miracles	Thomas Paine, one of the Founding Fathers of the American Revolution, wrote 'All the tales of Miracles with which the Old and New Testament are filled, are fit only for impostors to preach and fools to believe'. Thomas Jefferson, principle author of the Declaration of Independence, edited a version of the Bible in which he removed sections of the New Testament containing supernatural aspects as well as perceived misinterpretations he believed had been added by the Four Evangelists. Jefferson wrote, 'The establishment of the innocent and genuine character of this benevolent moralist, and the rescuing it from the imputation of imposture, which has resulted from artificial systems, [footnote: e.g. The immaculate conception of Jesus, his deification, the creation of the world by him, his miraculous powers, his resurrection and visible ascension, his corporeal presence in the Eucharist, the Trinity; original sin, atonement, regeneration, election, orders of Hierarchy, etc.
Social change	Social change refers to an alteration in the social order of a society. It may refer to the notion of social progress or sociocultural evolution, the philosophical idea that society moves forward by dialectical or evolutionary means. It may refer to a paradigmatic change in the socio-economic structure, for instance a shift away from feudalism and towards capitalism.
Theory	In mathematical logic, a theory (also called a formal theory) is a set of sentences in a formal language. Usually a deductive system is understood from context. An element $\phi \in T$ of a theory T is then called an axiom of the theory, and any sentence that follows from the axioms (

6. Sex and the Bodies of Religion: Seed and Soil

Oedipus complex	In psychoanalytic theory, the term Oedipus complex denotes the emotions and ideas that the mind keeps in the unconscious, via dynamic repression, that concentrate upon a boy's desire to sexually possess his mother, and kill his father. In the course of his psychosexual development, the complex is the boy's phallic stage formation of a discrete sexual identity; a girl's analogous experience is the Electra complex. The Oedipus complex occurs in the third -- phallic stage (ages 3 -6) -- of five psychosexual development stages: (i) the Oral, (ii) the Anal, (iii) the Phallic, (iv) the Latent, and (v) the Genital -- in which the source libido pleasure is in a different erogenous zone of the infant's body.
Institution	The notion of institution has been created by Joseph Goguen and Rod Burstall in the late 1970s in order to deal with the 'population explosion among the logical systems used in computer science'. The notion tries to capture the essence of the concept of 'logical system'. With this, it is possible to develop concepts of specification languages (like structuring of specifications, parameterization, implementation, refinement, development), proof calculi and even tools in a way completely independent of the underlying logical system.
Jerusalem	Jerusalem is the title of a book written by Moses Mendelssohn, which was first published in 1783 - the same year, when the Prussian officer Christian Wilhelm von Dohm published the second part of his Mémoire Concerning the amelioration of the civil status of the Jews. Moses Mendelssohn was one of the key figures of Jewish Enlightenment (Haskalah) and his philosophical treatise, dealing with social contract and political theory (especially concerning the question of the separation between religion and state), can be regarded as his most important contribution to Haskalah. The book which was written in Prussia on the eve of the French Revolution, consisted of two parts and each one was paged separately.
Torah	The term 'Torah' , refers either to the Five Books of Moses or to the entirety of Judaism's founding legal and ethical religious texts. A 'Sefer Torah' (×¡Öµ×¤Ö¶×¨ ×ªÖ¼×•Ö¹×¨Ö¸×", 'book of Torah') or Torah scroll, is a copy of the Torah written on parchment in a formal, traditional manner by a specially trained scribe under very strict requirements.

The Torah is the first of three parts of the Tanakh , the founding religious document of Judaism, Messiannic, and Hebrew belief, and is divided into five books, whose names in English are Genesis, Exodus, Leviticus, Numbers, and Deuteronomy, in reference to their themes . |
| Religious law | Religious law refers to ethical and moral codes taught by religious traditions. Examples include customary halakha (Jewish law), Hindu law, sharia (Islamic law) and Canon law (Christian law).

The two most prominent systems, canon law and shari'a, differ from other religious laws in that Canon law is the codification of Catholic, Anglican and Orthodox law as in civil law, while shari'a derives many of its laws from juristic precedent and reasoning by analogy (like in a common law tradition). |

6. Sex and the Bodies of Religion: Seed and Soil

Sharia	Sharia law is the moral code and religious law of Islam. Sharia deals with many topics addressed by secular law, including crime, politics and economics, as well as personal matters such as sexual intercourse, hygiene, diet, prayer, and fasting. Though interpretations of sharia vary between cultures, in its strictest definition it is considered the infallible law of God--as opposed to the human interpretation of the laws (fiqh).
Canon law	The canon law of the Catholic Church is a fully developed legal system, with all the necessary elements: courts, lawyers, judges, a fully articulated legal code and principles of legal interpretation. It lacks the necessary binding force present in most modern day legal systems. The academic degrees in canon law are the J.C.B. (Juris Canonici Baccalaureatus, Bachelor of Canon Law, normally taken as a graduate degree), J.C.L. (Juris Canonici Licentiatus, Licentiate of Canon Law) and the J.C.D. (Juris Canonici Doctor, Doctor of Canon Law).
Confucianism	Confucianism is a Chinese ethical and philosophical system developed from the teachings of the Chinese philosopher Confucius . Confucianism originated as an 'ethical-sociopolitical teaching' during the Spring and Autumn Period, but later developed metaphysical and cosmological elements in the Han Dynasty. Following the abandonment of Legalism in China after the Qin Dynasty, Confucianism became the official state ideology of China, until it was replaced by the 'Three Principles of the People' ideology with the establishment of the Republic of China, and then Maoist Communism after the ROC was replaced by the People's Republic of China in Mainland China.
Last Judgment	The concept of a Last Judgment is found in all Abrahamic religions and elsewhere like Zoroastrianism and Duat. In Islam, the Last Judgment is referred as Qiyamah and called a number of things, including 'the Day of Standing' and God Almighty, will judge all Creation. In Christian theology, the Last Judgment, Final Judgment, Judgment Day, or Day of the Lord is the final and eternal judgment by God of all nations.
Ernst Bergmann	Ernst Bergmann (7 August 1881, Colditz, Kingdom of Saxony - 16 April 1945, Naumburg) was a German philosopher and proponent of Nazism. He studied philosophy and German philology at the University of Leipzig and got his PhD in 1905. Subsequently he continued his studies in Berlin. Later he returned to Leipzig, where he received the status of Privatdozent at the university in 1911. In 1916 he was awarded the position of Ausserordentlicher Professor (professor without chair).
Belief	Belief is the psychological state in which an individual holds a proposition or premise to be true. The terms belief and knowledge are used differently in philosophy.

Perspective	Perspective in theory of cognition is the choice of a context or a reference from which to sense, categorize, measure or codify experience, cohesively forming a coherent belief, typically for comparing with another. One may further recognize a number of subtly distinctive meanings, close to those of paradigm, point of view, reality tunnel, umwelt, or weltanschauung.
	To choose a perspective is to choose a value system and, unavoidably, an associated belief system.
Sociology	Sociology is the study of human social behavior and its origins, development, organizations, and institutions. It is a social science which uses various methods of empirical investigation and critical analysis to develop a body of knowledge about human social actions, social structure and functions. A goal for many sociologists is to conduct research which may be applied directly to social policy and welfare, while others focus primarily on refining the theoretical understanding of social processes.
Protestantism	Protestantism is a branch within Christianity, containing many denominations of different practices and doctrines, that originated in the sixteenth-century Protestant Reformation. It is considered to be one of the primary divisions within the original Christian church, i.e., the Catholic Church, along with Eastern Orthodoxy. Some groups that are often loosely labeled 'Protestant' do not use the term to define themselves, and some tend to reject it because of the implication of being non-traditional.
Sect	Sect is an ancient astrological concept in which the seven traditional 'planets' (including the Sun, the Moon and the five starry planets) are assigned to two different categories: diurnal or nocturnal Sect.
	Diurnal planets are more comfortable and powerful when they appear in charts in which the Sun is above the horizon. They include:
	· Sun · Jupiter · Saturn
	Nocturnal planets are more comfortable and powerful when they appear in charts in which the Sun is below the horizon, or at night.
John Calvin	John Calvin was an influential French theologian and pastor during the Protestant Reformation. He was a principal figure in the development of the system of Christian theology later called Calvinism. Originally trained as a humanist lawyer, he broke from the Roman Catholic Church around 1530. After religious tensions provoked a violent uprising against Protestants in France, Calvin fled to Basel, Switzerland, where in 1536 he published the first edition of his seminal work Institutes of the Christian Religion.
Meister Eckhart	Eckhart von Hochheim O.P. (c. 1260 - c.

1327), commonly known as Meister Eckhart, was a German theologian, philosopher and mystic, born near Gotha, in the Landgraviate of Thuringia in the Holy Roman Empire. Meister is German for 'Master', referring to the academic title Magister in theologia he obtained in Paris. Coming into prominence during the Avignon Papacy and a time of increased tensions between the Franciscans and Eckhart's Dominican Order of Friars Preachers, he was brought up on charges later in life before the local Franciscan-led Inquisition.

Gopnik	Gopnik is a stereotypical class of young males up to 30 years old found in Russia and post-Soviet countries, characterized by aggressive behavior, specifically towards the weak, a predilection to the Blat criminal subculture, abuse of alcohol beverages (specifically beer, vodka and 'Jaguar' cocktail) and specific fashion preferences. Gopniks have been compared to the Chavs and Neds of the United Kingdom

The term 'gopnik' was probably derived from slang term gop-stop, meaning street mugging. Another theory is that 'gopnik' derived from the acronym GOP, probably a reference to Gorodskoye Obshchestvo Prizreniya (the City Society of Charity), the numerous almshouses organized by the government after the October Revolution. |
| Spiritual But Not Religious | Spiritual But Not Religious is a popular phrase and acronym used to self-identify a life stance of spirituality that rejects traditional organized religion as the sole or most valuable means of furthering spiritual growth. The term is used world-wide, but seems most prominent in the United States where one study reports that as many as 33% of people identify as spiritual but not religious. Other surveys report lower percentages ranging from 24%-10%

Those that identify as SBNR vary in their individual spiritual philosophies and practices and theological references. |
| Agnosticism | Agnosticism is the view that the truth values of certain claims--especially claims about the existence or non-existence of any deity, but also other religious and metaphysical claims--are unknown or unknowable. Agnosticism can be defined in various ways, and is sometimes used to indicate doubt or a skeptical approach to questions. In some senses, agnosticism is a stance about the difference between belief and knowledge, rather than about any specific claim or belief. |
| Materialism | In philosophy, the theory of materialism holds that the only thing that exists is matter or energy; that all things are composed of material and all phenomena (including consciousness) are the result of material interactions. In other words, matter is the only substance, and reality is identical with the actually occurring states of energy and matter.

To many philosophers, 'materialism' is synonymous with 'physicalism'. |
| Paranormal | Paranormal is a general term that describes unusual experiences that supposedly lack a scientific explanation, or phenomena alleged to be outside of science's current ability to explain or measure. |

	Notably, Paranormal phenomena also lack scientific evidence, as detectable but not well explained phenomena such as dark matter or dark energy are not commonly called Paranormal.
	In parapsychology, the term has, in the past, been used to describe the supposed phenomena of extra-sensory perception, including telepathy, and psychokinesis, ghosts, and hauntings.
Representation	Representation is the use of signs that stand in for and take the place of something else. It is through representation that people organize the world and reality through the act of naming its elements. Signs are arranged in order to form semantic constructions and express relations.
Skepticism	Skepticism, but generally refers to any questioning attitude towards knowledge, facts, or opinions/beliefs stated as facts, or doubt regarding claims that are taken for granted elsewhere. The word may characterize a position on a single matter, as in the case of religious skepticism, which is 'doubt concerning basic religious principles (such as immortality, providence, and revelation)', but philosophical skepticism is an overall approach that requires all information to be well supported by evidence. Skeptics may even doubt the reliability of their own senses.
Spiritualism	Spiritualism is a dualist metaphysical belief that the world is made up of at least two fundamental substances, matter and spirit. This very broad metaphysical distinction is further developed into many and various forms by the inclusion of details about what spiritual entities exist such as a soul, the afterlife, spirits of the dead, deities and mediums; as well as details about the nature of the relationship between spirit and matter. It may also refer to the philosophy, doctrine, or religion pertaining to a spiritual aspect of existence.
Charles Robert Darwin	Charles Robert Darwin FRS (12 February 1809 - 19 April 1882) was an English naturalist who established that all species of life have descended over time from common ancestors, and proposed the scientific theory that this branching pattern of evolution resulted from a process that he called natural selection. He published his theory with compelling evidence for evolution in his 1859 book On the Origin of Species. The scientific community and much of the general public came to accept evolution as a fact in his lifetime, but it was not until the emergence of the modern evolutionary synthesis from the 1930s to the 1950s that a broad consensus developed that natural selection was the basic mechanism of evolution.

6. Sex and the Bodies of Religion: Seed and Soil

1. An _____ is a person or agency considered to be a source of wise counsel or prophetic opinion. It may also be a revealed prediction or precognition of the future, from deities, that is spoken through another object or life-form (e.g.: augury and auspice).

    In the ancient world many sites gained a reputation for the dispensing of oracular wisdom: they too became known as '_____s,' and the oracular utterances, called khrÄ"smoi in Greek, were often referred to under the same name--a name derived from the Latin verb ÅrÄre, to speak.

    a. Ornithomancy
    b. Uromancy
    c. Oracle
    d. Axinomancy

2. _____, also spelled Kabala or Cabala, is an esoteric method, discipline and school of thought. Its definition varies according to the tradition and aims of those following it, from its religious origin as an integral part of Judaism, to Christian, New Age, or Occultist syncretic adaptions. _____ is a set of esoteric teachings meant to explain the relationship between an unchanging, eternal and mysterious Ein Sof (no end) and the mortal and finite universe (his creation).

    a. Kaddish
    b. Kabbalah
    c. Messianic Age
    d. Mosaic covenant

3. _____ from the Ancient Greek, ?κ-στασις (ek-stasis), is a subjective experience of total involvement of the subject, with an object of his or her awareness. Total involvement with an object of interest is not an ordinary experience because of being aware of other objects, thus _____ is an example of an altered state of consciousness characterized by diminished awareness of other objects or the total lack of the awareness of surroundings and everything around the object. For instance, if one is concentrating on a physical task, then one might cease to be aware of any intellectual thoughts.

    a. Erotic art
    b. Escapism
    c. Eyesore
    d. Ecstasy

4. . _____ were, according to the Book of Genesis, the first man and woman created by YHWH . In theology and in folklore studies, the technical term 'protoplasts' is sometimes used for the first humans in this sense.

    Narrative

    Genesis 2

    Genesis 2 opens with God fashioning a man from the dust and blowing life into his nostrils.

a. Henryk Batuta hoax
b. Adam and Eve
c. Minnesota Twin Family Study
d. Yadavas

5. _____ as a term of fine art refers to the posture or gesture given to a figure by a painter or sculptor. It applies to the body and not to a mental state, but the arrangement of the body is presumed to serve a communicative or expressive purpose. An example of a conventional _____ in art is proskynesis to indicate respect toward God, emperors, clerics of high status, and religious icons; in Byzantine art, it is particularly characteristic in depictions of the emperor paying homage to Christ.

a. ADD model
b. Renaissance philosophy
c. Attitude
d. Stephen William Hawking

1. c

2. b

3. d

4. b

5. c

You can take the complete Chapter Practice Test

for 6. Sex and the Bodies of Religion: Seed and Soil
on all key terms, persons, places, and concepts.

Online 99 Cents

http://www.JustTheFacts101.com

Use www.JustTheFacts101.com for all your study needs

including Facts101's online interactive problem solving labs in

chemistry, statistics, mathematics, and more.

CHAPTER OUTLINE: KEY TERMS, PEOPLE, PLACES, CONCEPTS

Terence McKenna

Reflexivity

Imagination

Religious experience

Revelation

Purity

Paranormal

Poltergeist

Skepticism

Trickster

Demon

Gospel

Miracles

Theory

Aristophanes

Mysticism

Philosophical analysis

Plato

Aristotle

Hermeneutics

Metaphor

	Representation
	Telepathy
	Sufi
	Liberation theology
	Theology
	Belief
	Demonology
	Mothman
	Polytheism
	Sleep paralysis
	Ernst Bergmann
	Fraud

CHAPTER HIGHLIGHTS & NOTES: KEY TERMS, PEOPLE, PLACES, CONCEPTS

Terence McKenna	Terence Kemp McKenna (November 16, 1946 - April 3, 2000) was an American philosopher, psychonaut, researcher, teacher, lecturer and writer on many subjects, such as human consciousness, language, psychedelic drugs, the evolution of civilizations, the origin and end of the universe, alchemy, and extraterrestrial beings. Early life
	Terence McKenna grew up in Paonia, Colorado. He was introduced to geology through his uncle and developed a hobby of solitary fossil hunting in the arroyos near his home.
Reflexivity	Reflexivity refers to circular relationships between cause and effect. A reflexive relationship is bidirectional with both the cause and the effect affecting one another in a situation that does not render both functions causes and effects.

7. Charisma and the Social Dimensions of Religion: Transmitting the Power ...

117

Imagination	Imagination, is the ability of forming images and sensations when they are not perceived through sight, hearing, or other senses. Imagination helps provide meaning to experience and understanding to knowledge; it is a fundamental faculty through which people make sense of the world, and it also plays a key role in the learning process. A basic training for imagination is listening to storytelling (narrative), in which the exactness of the chosen words is the fundamental factor to 'evoke worlds'.
Religious experience	A religious experience is a subjective experience in which an individual reports contact with a transcendent reality, an encounter or union with the divine. Such an experience often involves arriving at some knowledge or insight previously unavailable to the subject yet unaccountable or unforseeable according to the usual conceptual or psychological framework within which the subject has been used to operating. Religious experience generally brings understanding, partial or complete, of issues of a fundamental character that may have been a cause (whether consciously ackowledged or not) of anguish or alienation to the subject for an extended period of time.
Revelation	In religion and theology, revelation is the revealing or disclosing, through active or passive communication with a divine entity or entities. In general usage, the term is used to refer to the process by which God reveals knowledge of himself, his will, and his divine providence, to the world of human beings. In secondary usage, it refers to the resulting human knowledge about God, prophecy, and other divine things.
Purity	Purity (suddha) is an important concept within much of Theravada and Mahayana Buddhism, although the implications of the resultant moral purification may be viewed differently in the varying traditions. The aim is to purify the personality of the Buddhist practitioner so that all moral and character defilements and defects (kleshas such as anger, ignorance and lust) are wiped away and Nirvana can be obtained. Theravada Buddhism regards the path of self-purification as absolutely vital for the reaching of nibbana/nirvana.
Paranormal	Paranormal is a general term that describes unusual experiences that supposedly lack a scientific explanation, or phenomena alleged to be outside of science's current ability to explain or measure. Notably, Paranormal phenomena also lack scientific evidence, as detectable but not well explained phenomena such as dark matter or dark energy are not commonly called Paranormal. In parapsychology, the term has, in the past, been used to describe the supposed phenomena of extra-sensory perception, including telepathy, and psychokinesis, ghosts, and hauntings.
Poltergeist	In folklore and the paranormal, a poltergeist is the apparent manifestation of an imperceptible but noisy, disruptive or destructive entity. Most accounts of poltergeist manifestations involve noises and destruction that have no apparent cause.

7. Charisma and the Social Dimensions of Religion: Transmitting the Power ...

CHAPTER HIGHLIGHTS & NOTES: KEY TERMS, PEOPLE, PLACES, CONCEPTS

Skepticism	Skepticism, but generally refers to any questioning attitude towards knowledge, facts, or opinions/beliefs stated as facts, or doubt regarding claims that are taken for granted elsewhere. The word may characterize a position on a single matter, as in the case of religious skepticism, which is 'doubt concerning basic religious principles (such as immortality, providence, and revelation)', but philosophical skepticism is an overall approach that requires all information to be well supported by evidence. Skeptics may even doubt the reliability of their own senses.
Trickster	In mythology, and in the study of folklore and religion, a trickster is a god, goddess, spirit, man, woman, or anthropomorphic animal who plays tricks or otherwise disobeys normal rules and conventional behavior. It is suggested by Hansen (2001) that the term 'Trickster' was probably first used in this context by Daniel G. Brinton in 1885. Mythology The trickster deity breaks the rules of the gods or nature, sometimes maliciously (for example, Loki) but usually, albeit unintentionally, with ultimately positive effects.
Demon	A demon is a supernatural, often malevolent being prevalent in religion, occultism, literature, and folklore. The original Greek word daimon does not carry the negative connotation initially understood by implementation of the Koine δαιμ?νιον (daimonion), and later ascribed to any cognate words sharing the root. In Ancient Near Eastern religions as well as in the Abrahamic traditions, including ancient and medieval Christian demonology, a demon is considered an 'unclean spirit' which may cause demonic possession, calling for an exorcism.
Gospel	A Gospel is a writing that describes the life of Jesus. The word is primarily used to refer to the four canonical Gospels: the Gospel of Matthew, Gospel of Mark, Gospel of Luke and Gospel of John, probably written between AD 65 and 80. They appear to have been originally untitled; they were quoted anonymously in the first half of the second century (i.e. 100-150) but the names by which they are currently known appear suddenly around the year 180. The first canonical Gospel written is thought by most scholars to be Mark (c 65-70), which was according to the majority used as a source for the Gospels of Matthew and Luke.
Miracles	Thomas Paine, one of the Founding Fathers of the American Revolution, wrote 'All the tales of Miracles with which the Old and New Testament are filled, are fit only for impostors to preach and fools to believe'. Thomas Jefferson, principle author of the Declaration of Independence, edited a version of the Bible in which he removed sections of the New Testament containing supernatural aspects as well as perceived misinterpretations he believed had been added by the Four Evangelists.

7. Charisma and the Social Dimensions of Religion: Transmitting the Power ...

119

CHAPTER HIGHLIGHTS & NOTES: KEY TERMS, PEOPLE, PLACES, CONCEPTS

	Jefferson wrote, 'The establishment of the innocent and genuine character of this benevolent moralist, and the rescuing it from the imputation of imposture, which has resulted from artificial systems, [footnote: e.g. The immaculate conception of Jesus, his deification, the creation of the world by him, his miraculous powers, his resurrection and visible ascension, his corporeal presence in the Eucharist, the Trinity; original sin, atonement, regeneration, election, orders of Hierarchy, etc.
Theory	In mathematical logic, a theory (also called a formal theory) is a set of sentences in a formal language. Usually a deductive system is understood from context. An element $\phi \in T$ of a theory T is then called an axiom of the theory, and any sentence that follows from the axioms ($T \vdash \phi$) is called a theorem of the theory.
Aristophanes	Aristophanes, son of Philippus, of the deme Cydathenaus, was a prolific and much acclaimed comic playwright of ancient Athens. Eleven of his forty plays survive virtually complete. These, together with fragments of some of his other plays, provide us with the only real examples we have of a genre of comic drama known as Old Comedy, and they are in fact used to define the genre.
Mysticism	Mysticism is the pursuit of communion with, identity with divinity, spiritual truth intuition, instinct or insight. Mysticism usually centers on a practice or practices intended to nurture those experiences or awareness. Mysticism may be dualistic, maintaining a distinction between the self and the divine, or may be nondualistic.
Philosophical analysis	Philosophical analysis is a general term for techniques typically used by philosophers in the analytic tradition that involve 'breaking down' (i.e. analyzing) philosophical issues.
Plato	Plato was a Classical Greek philosopher, mathematician, student of Socrates, writer of philosophical dialogues, and founder of the Academy in Athens, the first institution of higher learning in the Western world. Along with his mentor, Socrates, and his student, Aristotle, Plato helped to lay the foundations of Western philosophy and science. In the words of A. N. Whitehead:' The safest general characterization of the European philosophical tradition is that it consists of a series of footnotes to Plato.'
Aristotle	Aristotle was a Greek philosopher and polymath, a student of Plato and teacher of Alexander the Great. His writings cover many subjects, including physics, metaphysics, poetry, theater, music, logic, rhetoric, linguistics, politics, government, ethics, biology, and zoology. Together with Plato and Socrates (Plato's teacher), Aristotle is one of the most important founding figures in Western philosophy.
Hermeneutics	In religious studies and social philosophy, hermeneutics is the study of the theory and practice of interpretation.

7. Charisma and the Social Dimensions of Religion: Transmitting the Power ...

CHAPTER HIGHLIGHTS & NOTES: KEY TERMS, PEOPLE, PLACES, CONCEPTS

	Traditional hermeneutics is the study of the interpretation of written texts, especially texts in the areas of literature, religion and law. A type of traditional hermeneutic is Biblical hermeneutics which concerns the study of the interpretation of The Bible.
Metaphor	A metaphor is a literary figure of speech that describes a subject by asserting that it is, on some point of comparison, the same as another otherwise unrelated object. Metaphor is a type of analogy and is closely related to other rhetorical figures of speech that achieve their effects via association, comparison or resemblance including allegory, hyperbole, and simile. One of the most prominent examples of a metaphor in English literature is the All the world's a stage monologue from As You Like It:All the world's a stage,And all the men and women merely players;They have their exits and their entrances; -- William Shakespeare, As You Like It, 2/7 This quote is a metaphor because the world is not literally a stage.
Representation	Representation is the use of signs that stand in for and take the place of something else. It is through representation that people organize the world and reality through the act of naming its elements. Signs are arranged in order to form semantic constructions and express relations.
Telepathy	Telepathy , is the ostensible transfer of information on thoughts or feelings between individuals by means other than the five senses. The term was coined in 1882 by the classical scholar Fredric W. H. Myers, a founder of the Society for Psychical Research, specifically to replace the earlier expression thought-transference.
Sufi	The lexical root of Sufi is variously traced to ØµÙÙˆÙ á¹£Å«f 'wool', referring either to the simple cloaks the early Muslim ascetics wore, or possibly to ØµÙÙŽÙØ§Ø§ á¹£afÄ 'purity'. The two were combined by al-Rudhabari who said, 'The Sufi is the one who wears wool on top of purity.' The wool cloaks were sometimes a designation of their initiation into the Sufi order. The early Sufi orders considered the wearing of this coat an imitation of Isa bin Maryam (Jesus).
Liberation theology	Liberation theology is a political movement in Christian theology which interprets the teachings of Jesus Christ in terms of a liberation from unjust economic, political, or social conditions. It has been described by proponents as 'an interpretation of Christian faith through the poor's suffering, their struggle and hope, and a critique of society and the Catholic faith and Christianity through the eyes of the poor', and by detractors as Christianized Marxism. Although liberation theology has grown into an international and inter-denominational movement, it began as a movement within the Roman Catholic church in Latin America in the 1950s-1960s.

7. Charisma and the Social Dimensions of Religion: Transmitting the Power ...

121

Theology	Theology is the rational and systematic study of religion and its influences and of the nature of religious truth, or the learned profession acquired by specialized courses in religion, usually taught at a college or seminary. Augustine of Hippo defined the Latin equivalent, theologia, as 'reasoning or discussion concerning the Deity'; Richard Hooker defined 'theology' in English as 'the science of things divine'. The term can, however, be used for a variety of different disciplines or forms of discourse.
Belief	Belief is the psychological state in which an individual holds a proposition or premise to be true. The terms belief and knowledge are used differently in philosophy. Epistemology is the philosophical study of knowledge and belief.
Demonology	Demonology is the systematic study of demons or beliefs about demons. It is the branch of theology relating to superhuman beings who are not gods. It deals both with benevolent beings that have no circle of worshippers or so limited a circle as to be below the rank of gods, and with malevolent beings of all kinds.
Mothman	The Mothman is a creature reportedly seen in the Charleston and Point Pleasant areas of West Virginia from November 12, 1966, to December 1967. Most observers describe the Mothman as a winged man-sized creature with large reflective red eyes and large moth-like wings. The creature was sometimes reported as having no head, with its eyes set into its chest.
Polytheism	Polytheism is the belief in and worship of multiple deities, called gods and goddesses. These are usually assembled into a pantheon, along with their own mythologies and rituals. Many religions, both historical and contemporary, have a belief in Polytheism, such as Hinduism, Buddhism, Shinto, Ancient Greek Polytheism, Roman Polytheism, Germanic Polytheism, Slavic Polytheism, Chinese folk religion, Neopagan faiths and Anglo-Saxon paganism.
Sleep paralysis	Sleep paralysis is paralysis associated with sleep that may occur in healthy persons or may be associated with narcolepsy, cataplexy, and hypnagogic hallucinations. The pathophysiology of this condition is closely related to the normal hypotonia that occurs during REM sleep. When considered to be a disease, isolated sleep paralysis is classified as MeSH D020188. Some evidence suggests that it can also, in some cases, be a symptom of migraine.
Ernst Bergmann	Ernst Bergmann (7 August 1881, Colditz, Kingdom of Saxony - 16 April 1945, Naumburg) was a German philosopher and proponent of Nazism. He studied philosophy and German philology at the University of Leipzig and got his PhD in 1905. Subsequently he continued his studies in Berlin. Later he returned to Leipzig, where he received the status of Privatdozent at the university in 1911.

7. Charisma and the Social Dimensions of Religion: Transmitting the Power ...

Fraud	In criminal law, a fraud is an intentional deception made for personal gain or to damage another individual; the related adjective is fraudulent. The specific legal definition varies by legal jurisdiction. Fraud is a crime, and also a civil law violation.

1. _____, son of Philippus, of the deme Cydathenaus, was a prolific and much acclaimed comic playwright of ancient Athens. Eleven of his forty plays survive virtually complete. These, together with fragments of some of his other plays, provide us with the only real examples we have of a genre of comic drama known as Old Comedy, and they are in fact used to define the genre.

   a. Aristophanes
   b. Epicurus
   c. ADD model
   d. Religious philosophy

2. _____ is the pursuit of communion with, identity with divinity, spiritual truth intuition, instinct or insight. _____ usually centers on a practice or practices intended to nurture those experiences or awareness. _____ may be dualistic, maintaining a distinction between the self and the divine, or may be nondualistic.

   a. Philosophy of religion
   b. Mysticism
   c. The British Society for the Philosophy of Religion
   d. Credo ut intelligam

3. _____ refers to circular relationships between cause and effect. A reflexive relationship is bidirectional with both the cause and the effect affecting one another in a situation that does not render both functions causes and effects. In sociology, _____ therefore comes to mean an act of self-reference where examination or action 'bends back on', refers to, and affects the entity instigating the action or examination.

   a. Relative deprivation
   b. Reflexivity
   c. Reverse psychology
   d. Rule complex

4. . _____ is the belief in and worship of multiple deities, called gods and goddesses. These are usually assembled into a pantheon, along with their own mythologies and rituals.

Many religions, both historical and contemporary, have a belief in _____, such as Hinduism, Buddhism, Shinto, Ancient Greek _____, Roman _____, Germanic _____, Slavic _____, Chinese folk religion, Neopagan faiths and Anglo-Saxon paganism.

a. Philosophy of religion
b. The Name of the Rose
c. Polytheism
d. Credo ut intelligam

5. Terence Kemp McKenna (November 16, 1946 - April 3, 2000) was an American philosopher, psychonaut, researcher, teacher, lecturer and writer on many subjects, such as human consciousness, language, psychedelic drugs, the evolution of civilizations, the origin and end of the universe, alchemy, and extraterrestrial beings. Early life

    _____ grew up in Paonia, Colorado. He was introduced to geology through his uncle and developed a hobby of solitary fossil hunting in the arroyos near his home.

    a. Penelope Maddy
    b. Terence McKenna
    c. Nicholas Maxwell
    d. Lee C. McIntyre

1. a
2. b
3. b
4. c
5. b

You can take the complete Chapter Practice Test

for 7. Charisma and the Social Dimensions of Religion: Transmitting the Power ...
on all key terms, persons, places, and concepts.

Online 99 Cents

http://www.JustTheFacts101.com

Use www.JustTheFacts101.com for all your study needs

including Facts101's online interactive problem solving labs in

chemistry, statistics, mathematics, and more.

8. The Final Questions of Soul, Salvation, and the End of All Things: The ...

Friedrich

Nietzsche

Society

Consciousness

Soul

Mysticism

Philosophical analysis

Swami Niranjanananda

Kashmir Shaivism

Buddhism

Sikhism

Reincarnation

Salvation

Neoplatonism

Renaissance

Afterlife

Avatar

Shamanism

Theology

Daoism

Egyptian

8. The Final Questions of Soul, Salvation, and the End of All Things: The ...

127

CHAPTER OUTLINE: KEY TERMS, PEOPLE, PLACES, CONCEPTS

Belief

Descartes

Protestantism

Animism

Colonialism

Panpsychism

Religious experience

Skepticism

William Blake

I Ching

Spinoza

Iconoclasm

Representation

Spirit possession

Spiritualism

Cicero

Kenneth Wapnick

Agnosticism

Atheism

Clairvoyance

Cremation

Perennial philosophy

Dissociation

Jainism

Tantra

Transcendence

Yoga

Eschatology

Emperor

Revelation

Apocalypse

Expression

Myth and ritual

Piety

Violence

Hermes Trismegistus

Sharia

Near-death experience

Terrorism

Plato

Republic

Padmasambhava

8. The Final Questions of Soul, Salvation, and the End of All Things: The ...

129

Life After Life

Purity

Telepathy

Paranormal

Embraced by the Light

Exclusivism

History of religions

Stoicism

Reflexivity

Akbar

Voltaire

Ralph Waldo Emerson

Authority

Perception

Apologetics

Polemic

Creation myth

Universality

Inclusivism

Contextualism

Conversion

8. The Final Questions of Soul, Salvation, and the End of All Things: The ...

CHAPTER OUTLINE: KEY TERMS, PEOPLE, PLACES, CONCEPTS

	Damnation
	Theory
	Ernst Bergmann
	Dilemma
	Sociology
	Nostra Aetate
	Quran
	Buddha
	Vishnu
	Caste
	Spiritual But Not Religious
	World Religions
	EPIC
	Civil Rights
	Equality
	Justice
	Liberation theology
	Social justice
	Criticism
	Historical criticism
	Black theology

8. The Final Questions of Soul, Salvation, and the End of All Things: The ...

131

CHAPTER OUTLINE: KEY TERMS, PEOPLE, PLACES, CONCEPTS

	Patriarchy
	Feminist theology
	Suffrage
	Queer theology
	Womanist theology
	Judith Butler
	Homosexuality
	Celibacy
	Ambedkar
	Dalit

CHAPTER HIGHLIGHTS & NOTES: KEY TERMS, PEOPLE, PLACES, CONCEPTS

Friedrich	The Friedrich are the most ancient German-Bohemian glass-maker family.
	History
	From as early as 750 years ago, the shadowy picture of the oldest German-Bohemian glass-maker family Friedrich emerges, who contributed greatly towards the creation of the world-famous Bohemian glass (also called Bohemian Crystal). In pre-Hussite times they produced amazing works of vitreous art near Daubitz, nowadays called Doubice.
Nietzsche	Friedrich Wilhelm Nietzsche was a 19th-century German philosopher and classical philologist. He wrote critical texts on religion, morality, contemporary culture, philosophy and science, using a distinctive German-language style and displaying a fondness for metaphor, irony and aphorism.

Society	A society, or a human society, is a group of people involved with each other through persistent relations, or a large social grouping sharing the same geographical or social territory, subject to the same political authority and dominant cultural expectations. Human societies are characterized by patterns of relationships (social relations) between individuals who share a distinctive culture and institutions; a given society may be described as the sum total of such relationships among its constituent members. In the social sciences, a larger society often evinces stratification and/or dominance patterns in subgroups.
Consciousness	Consciousness is the quality or state of being aware of an external object or something within oneself. It has been defined as: subjectivity, awareness, the ability to experience or to feel, wakefulness, having a sense of selfhood, and the executive control system of the mind. Despite the difficulty in definition, many philosophers believe that there is a broadly shared underlying intuition about what consciousness is.
Soul	The soul--in many traditional spiritual, philosophical, and psychological traditions--is the incorporeal and immortal essence of a person, living thing, or object. According to some religions (including the Abrahamic religions in most of their forms), souls--or at least immortal souls capable of union with the divine--belong only to human beings. For example, the Catholic theologian Thomas Aquinas attributed 'soul' (anima) to all organisms but taught that only human souls are immortal.
Mysticism	Mysticism is the pursuit of communion with, identity with divinity, spiritual truth intuition, instinct or insight. Mysticism usually centers on a practice or practices intended to nurture those experiences or awareness. Mysticism may be dualistic, maintaining a distinction between the self and the divine, or may be nondualistic.
Philosophical analysis	Philosophical analysis is a general term for techniques typically used by philosophers in the analytic tradition that involve 'breaking down' (i.e. analyzing) philosophical issues.
Swami Niranjanananda	Swami Niranjanananda (Senior) born as Nitya Niranjan Ghosh, usually called by the shortened name of Niranjan, was one of the foremost monks of Ramakrishna Mission and was one of the direct monastic disciples of Ramakrishna. Swami Niranjanananda was one of those few disciples,whom Sri Ramakrishna termed as 'Nityasiddhas' or 'Ishwarakotis' - that is, souls who are ever perfect. [Swami Niranjanananda (Senior)is termed Senior since there was another Swami Niranjanananda (Junior) also known as Pandalai Maharaj, later in the Ramakrishna Mission who died in 1972].
Kashmir Shaivism	Among the various Hindu philosophies, Kashmir Shaivism is a school of Saivism identical with trika Saivism categorized by various scholars as monistic idealism (absolute idealism, theistic monism, realistic idealism, transcendental physicalism or concrete monism). These descriptors denote a standpoint that Cit (consciousness) is the one reality.

8. The Final Questions of Soul, Salvation, and the End of All Things: The ...

133

Buddhism	Buddhism is a religion and philosophy indigenous to the Indian subcontinent that encompasses a variety of traditions, beliefs, and practices largely based on teachings attributed to Siddhartha Gautama, who is commonly known as the Buddha . The Buddha lived and taught in the eastern part of Indian subcontinent some time between the 6th and 4th centuries BCE. He is recognized by Buddhists as an awakened or enlightened teacher who shared his insights to help sentient beings end suffering (dukkha) through eliminating ignorance (avidya), craving , and hatred, by way of understanding and seeing dependent origination (pratityasamutpada) and non-self (anatman), and thus attain the highest happiness, nirvana (nirvana).
	Two major branches of Buddhism are recognized: Theravada ('The School of the Elders') and Mahayana ('The Great Vehicle').
Sikhism	Sikhism is a panentheistic religion founded during the 15th century in the Punjab region, by Guru Nanak Dev and continued to progress with ten successive Sikh gurus (the last teaching being the holy scripture Guru Granth Sahib Ji). It is the fifth-largest organized religion in the world, with over 30 million Sikhs and one of the most steadily growing. This system of religious philosophy and expression has been traditionally known as the Gurmat (literally 'wisdom of the Guru').
Reincarnation	Reincarnation is a 2008 fantasy novel by American author Suzanne Weyn. The novel was released on January 1, 2008. It tells the story of a two lovers who attempt to find each other through the centuries. The narrative follows the action through time.
Salvation	Salvation, in religion, is the saving of the soul from sin and its consequences. It may also be called 'deliverance' or 'redemption' from sin and its effects.
	Depending on the religious tradition, salvation is considered to be caused either by the free will and grace of a deity (in theistic religions) or by personal responsibility and self-effort (e.g. in the sramanic and yogic traditions of India).
Neoplatonism	Neoplatonism is the modern term for a school of mystical philosophy that took shape in the 3rd century AD, based on the teachings of Plato and earlier Platonists, with its earliest contributor believed to be Plotinus, and his teacher Ammonius Saccas. Neoplatonism focused on the spiritual and cosmological aspects of Platonic thought, synthesizing Platonism with Egyptian and Jewish theology. However, Neoplatonists would have considered themselves simply Platonists, and the modern distinction is due to the perception that their philosophy contained sufficiently unique interpretations of Plato to make it substantially different from what Plato wrote and believed.
Renaissance	The Renaissance was a cultural movement that spanned the period roughly from the 14th to the 17th century, beginning in Italy in the Late Middle Ages and later spreading to the rest of Europe. Though the invention of printing sped the dissemination of ideas from the later 15th century, the changes of the Renaissance were not uniformly experienced across Europe.

Afterlife	In philosophy, religion, mythology, and fiction, the afterlife is the concept of a realm, or the realm itself (whether physical or transcendental), in which an essential part of an individual's identity or consciousness continues to reside after the death of the body in the individual's lifetime. According to various ideas of the afterlife, the essential aspect of the individual that lives on after death may be some partial element, or the entire soul, of an individual, which carries with it and confers personal identity. Belief in an afterlife, which may be naturalistic or supernatural, is in contrast to the belief in eternal oblivion after death.
Avatar	In Hinduism, avatar, or a descent of the Supreme Being (i.e., Vishnu for Vaishnavites) and is mostly translated into English as 'incarnation', but more accurately as 'appearance' or 'manifestation'.
	The term is most often associated with Vishnu, though it has also come to be associated with other deities. Varying lists of avatars of Vishnu appear in Hindu scriptures, including the ten Dashavatara of the Garuda Purana and the twenty-two avatars in the Bhagavata Purana, though the latter adds that the incarnations of Vishnu are innumerable.
Shamanism	Shamanism is a term used in a variety of anthropological, historical and popular contexts to refer to certain magico-religious practices that involve a practitioner reaching altered states of consciousness in order to encounter and interact with the spirit world. A shaman is a person regarded as having access to, and influence in, the world of benevolent and malevolent spirits, who typically enters a trance state during a ritual, and practices divination and healing. The exact definition and use of the term 'shamanism' has been highly debated by scholars, with no clear consensus on the issue.
Theology	Theology is the rational and systematic study of religion and its influences and of the nature of religious truth, or the learned profession acquired by specialized courses in religion, usually taught at a college or seminary.
	Augustine of Hippo defined the Latin equivalent, theologia, as 'reasoning or discussion concerning the Deity'; Richard Hooker defined 'theology' in English as 'the science of things divine'. The term can, however, be used for a variety of different disciplines or forms of discourse.
Daoism	In English, the words Daoism and Taoism are the subject of an ongoing controversy over the preferred romanization for naming this native Chinese philosophy and Chinese religion. The root Chinese word é" 'way, path' is romanized tao in the older Wade-Giles system and dào in the modern Pinyin system. The sometimes heated arguments over Taoism vs. Daoism involve sinology, phonemes, loanwords, and politics - not to mention whether Taoism should be pronounced or .
Egyptian	Egyptians is the name of the nationality and Mediterranean North African ethnic group native to Egypt.

8. The Final Questions of Soul, Salvation, and the End of All Things: The ...

135

CHAPTER HIGHLIGHTS & NOTES: KEY TERMS, PEOPLE, PLACES, CONCEPTS

Egyptian identity is closely tied to the Geography of Egypt, dominated by the lower Nile Valley, the small strip of cultivable land stretching from the First Cataract to the Mediterranean Sea and enclosed by desert both to the east and to the west. This unique geography has been the basis of the development of Egyptian society since antiquity.

Belief	Belief is the psychological state in which an individual holds a proposition or premise to be true. The terms belief and knowledge are used differently in philosophy. Epistemology is the philosophical study of knowledge and belief.
Descartes	René Descartes also known as Renatus Cartesius , was a French philosopher, mathematician, physicist, and writer who spent most of his adult life in the Dutch Republic. He has been dubbed the 'Father of Modern Philosophy', and much of subsequent Western philosophy is a response to his writings, which continue to be studied closely to this day. In particular, his Meditations on First Philosophy continues to be a standard text at most university philosophy departments.
Protestantism	Protestantism is a branch within Christianity, containing many denominations of different practices and doctrines, that originated in the sixteenth-century Protestant Reformation. It is considered to be one of the primary divisions within the original Christian church, i.e., the Catholic Church, along with Eastern Orthodoxy. Some groups that are often loosely labeled 'Protestant' do not use the term to define themselves, and some tend to reject it because of the implication of being non-traditional.
Animism	Animism is a philosophical, religious or spiritual idea that souls or spirits exist not only in humans but also in other animals, plants, rocks, natural phenomena such as thunder, geographic features such as mountains or rivers a proposition also known as hylozoism in philosophy. Animism may further attribute souls to abstract concepts such as words, true names or metaphors in mythology. Religions which emphasize Animism are mostly folk religions, such as the various forms of Shamanism, but also Shinto and certain currents of Hinduism emphasize the concept.
Colonialism	Colonialism is the building and maintaining of colonies in one territory by people based elsewhere. Colonialism is a process whereby sovereignty over the colony is claimed by the metropole, who impose a new government and perhaps a new social structure and economy. Colonialism comprises unequal relationships between metropole and colony and between colonists and the indigenous population.
Panpsychism	In philosophy, panpsychism is the view that all matter has a mental aspect, or, alternatively, all objects have a unified center of experience or point of view. Baruch Spinoza, Gottfried Leibniz, Gustav Theodor Fechner, Friedrich Paulsen, Ernst Haeckel, Charles Strong, and partially William James are considered panpsychists.

Religious experience	A religious experience is a subjective experience in which an individual reports contact with a transcendent reality, an encounter or union with the divine. Such an experience often involves arriving at some knowledge or insight previously unavailable to the subject yet unaccountable or unforseeable according to the usual conceptual or psychological framework within which the subject has been used to operating. Religious experience generally brings understanding, partial or complete, of issues of a fundamental character that may have been a cause (whether consciously ackowledged or not) of anguish or alienation to the subject for an extended period of time.
Skepticism	Skepticism, but generally refers to any questioning attitude towards knowledge, facts, or opinions/beliefs stated as facts, or doubt regarding claims that are taken for granted elsewhere. The word may characterize a position on a single matter, as in the case of religious skepticism, which is 'doubt concerning basic religious principles (such as immortality, providence, and revelation)', but philosophical skepticism is an overall approach that requires all information to be well supported by evidence. Skeptics may even doubt the reliability of their own senses.
William Blake	William Blake (28 November 1757 - 12 August 1827) was an English poet, painter, and printmaker. Largely unrecognised during his lifetime, Blake is now considered a seminal figure in the history of both the poetry and visual arts of the Romantic Age. His prophetic poetry has been said to form 'what is in proportion to its merits the least read body of poetry in the English language'.
I Ching	The I Ching or 'Yì Jìng' (pinyin), also known as the Classic of Changes, Book of Changes and Zhouyi, is one of the oldest of the Chinese classic texts. The book contains a divination system comparable to Western geomancy or the West African Ifá system; in Western cultures and modern East Asia, it is still widely used for this purpose. Traditionally, the I Ching and its hexagrams were thought to pre-date recorded history, and based on traditional Chinese accounts, its origins trace back to the 3rd to the 2nd millennium BC. Modern scholarship suggests that the earliest layer of the text may date from the end of the 2nd millennium BC, but place doubts on the mythological aspects in the traditional accounts.
Spinoza	Baruch or Benedict de Spinoza was a Dutch philosopher of Portuguese Jewish origin. Revealing considerable scientific aptitude, the breadth and importance of Spinoza's work was not fully realized until years after his death. Today, he is considered one of the great rationalists of 17th-century philosophy, laying the groundwork for the 18th century Enlightenment and modern biblical criticism.
Iconoclasm	Iconoclasm is the deliberate destruction of religious icons and other symbols or monuments, usually with religious or political motives. It is a frequent component of major political or religious changes. The term encompasses the more specific destruction of images of a ruler after his death or overthrow (damnatio memoriae), for example, following Akhenaten's death in Ancient Egypt.
Representation	Representation is the use of signs that stand in for and take the place of something else.

8. The Final Questions of Soul, Salvation, and the End of All Things: The ...

137

CHAPTER HIGHLIGHTS & NOTES: KEY TERMS, PEOPLE, PLACES, CONCEPTS

	It is through representation that people organize the world and reality through the act of naming its elements. Signs are arranged in order to form semantic constructions and express relations.
Spirit possession	Spirit possession is a concept of paranormal, supernatural, psychological and/or superstitious belief in which spirits, gods, demons/daemons (demonic possession), animas, ET's or other disincarnate or extraterrestrial entities may take control of a human body, resulting in noticeable changes in health and behavior. The concept of spiritual possession exists in Christianity and other contemporary religions and can also be seen in the mythology, regression therapy and folklore of many cultures. One way that those who participate or practice Haitian Vodou and related traditions can have a spiritual experience is by being possessed by the lwa.
Spiritualism	Spiritualism is a dualist metaphysical belief that the world is made up of at least two fundamental substances, matter and spirit. This very broad metaphysical distinction is further developed into many and various forms by the inclusion of details about what spiritual entities exist such as a soul, the afterlife, spirits of the dead, deities and mediums; as well as details about the nature of the relationship between spirit and matter. It may also refer to the philosophy, doctrine, or religion pertaining to a spiritual aspect of existence.
Cicero	Marcus Tullius Cicero was a Roman philosopher, statesman, lawyer, orator, political theorist, Roman consul and constitutionalist. He came from a wealthy municipal family of the equestrian order, and is widely considered one of Rome's greatest orators and prose stylists. He introduced the Romans to the chief schools of Greek philosophy and created a Latin philosophical vocabulary (with neologisms such as humanitas, qualitas, quantitas, and essentia) distinguishing himself as a linguist, translator, and philosopher.
Kenneth Wapnick	Kenneth Wapnick, Ph.D. was born in 1942 in Brooklyn, New York. Together with Dr. William Thetford and scribe, Dr. Helen Schucman, Ken Wapnick helped edit the work known as A Course In Miracles. Educated as a psychologist, he currently heads the Foundation for A Course In Miracles (or FACIM).
Agnosticism	Agnosticism is the view that the truth values of certain claims--especially claims about the existence or non-existence of any deity, but also other religious and metaphysical claims--are unknown or unknowable. Agnosticism can be defined in various ways, and is sometimes used to indicate doubt or a skeptical approach to questions. In some senses, agnosticism is a stance about the difference between belief and knowledge, rather than about any specific claim or belief.
Atheism	Atheism is, in a broad sense, the rejection of belief in the existence of deities. In a narrower sense, atheism is specifically the position that there are no deities.

Clairvoyance	The term Clairvoyance is used to refer to the ability to gain information about an object, person, location or physical event through means other than the known human senses, a form of extra-sensory perception. A person said to have the ability of Clairvoyance is referred to as a clairvoyant . Claims for the existence of paranormal and psychic abilities such as Clairvoyance are highly controversial.
Cremation	Today, cremation is an increasingly popular form of disposition of the deceased. This is true even in the Christian world, which for many years was opposed to cremation, but has come to a greater acceptance of cremation over the past century. In Christian countries, cremation fell out of favour due to the Christian belief in the physical resurrection of the body, and as a mark of difference from the Iron Age European pre-Christian Pagan religions, which usually cremated their dead.
Perennial philosophy	Perennial philosophy is the notion of the universal recurrence of philosophical insight independent of epoch or culture, including universal truths on the nature of reality, humanity or consciousness (anthropological universals). The perennial philosophy is a perspective within the philosophy of religion which views each of the world's religious traditions as sharing a single, universal truth and a single divine foundation of all religious knowledge. Each world religion, independent of its cultural or historical context, is simply a different interpretation of this knowledge.
Dissociation	Dissociation is an unexpected partial or complete disruption of the normal integration of a person's conscious or psychological functioning. Dissociation is a mental process that severs a connection to a person's thoughts, memories, feelings, actions, or sense of identity. Dissociation can be a response to trauma, and perhaps allows the mind to distance itself from experiences that are too much for the psyche to process at that time.
Jainism	Jainism, is an Indian religion that prescribes a path of non-violence towards all living beings. Its philosophy and practice emphasize the necessity of self-effort to move the soul towards divine consciousness and liberation. Any soul that has conquered its own inner enemies and achieved the state of supreme being is called a jina ('conqueror' or 'victor').
Tantra	Tantra and the universe is regarded as the divine play of Shakti and Shiva. The word Tantra also applies to any of the scriptures (called 'Tantras') commonly identified with the worship of Shakti. Tantra deals primarily with spiritual practices and ritual forms of worship, which aim at liberation from ignorance and rebirth.

8. The Final Questions of Soul, Salvation, and the End of All Things: The ...

139

CHAPTER HIGHLIGHTS & NOTES: KEY TERMS, PEOPLE, PLACES, CONCEPTS

Transcendence	In religion, transcendence refers to the aspect of God's nature and power which is wholly independent of (and removed from) the material universe. This is contrasted with immanence where God is fully present in the physical world and thus accessible to creatures in various ways. In religious experience transcendence is a state of being that has overcome the limitations of physical existence and by some definitions has also become independent of it.
Yoga	Yoga refers to traditional physical and mental disciplines that originated in India. The word is associated with meditative practices in Hinduism, Buddhism and Jainism. Within Hinduism, it refers to one of the six orthodox (astika) schools of Hindu philosophy, and to the goal towards which that school directs its practices.
Eschatology	Eschatology is a part of theology, philosophy, and futurology concerned with what are believed to be the final events of history, the ultimate destiny of humanity--commonly referred to as the 'end of the world' or 'end time'. The Oxford English Dictionary defines eschatology as 'The department of theological science concerned with 'the four last things: death, judgement, heaven, and hell'.' In the context of mysticism, the phrase refers metaphorically to the end of ordinary reality and reunion with the Divine. In many religions it is taught as an existing future event prophesied in sacred texts or folklore.
Emperor	An emperor is a (male) monarch, usually the sovereign ruler of an empire or another type of imperial realm. Empress, the female equivalent, may indicate an emperor's wife (empress consort) or a woman who rules in her own right (empress regnant). Emperors are generally recognized to be of a higher honor and rank than kings.
Revelation	In religion and theology, revelation is the revealing or disclosing, through active or passive communication with a divine entity or entities. In general usage, the term is used to refer to the process by which God reveals knowledge of himself, his will, and his divine providence, to the world of human beings. In secondary usage, it refers to the resulting human knowledge about God, prophecy, and other divine things.
Apocalypse	An apocalypse is a revelation of something hidden. In religious contexts it is usually a revelation of hidden meaning - hidden from mankind in an era dominated by falsehood and misconception. In the Revelation of John, the last book of the New Testament, the revelation which John receives is that of the ultimate victory of good over evil and the end of the present age; and so some people have used the word apocalypse very loosely to refer to any End Time scenario, or to the end of the world in general.
Expression	In mathematics, an expression is a finite combination of symbols that is well-formed according to rules that depend on the context.

	Symbols can designate numbers (constants), variables, operations, functions, and other mathematical symbols, as well as punctuation, symbols of grouping, and other syntactic symbols. The use of expressions can range from the simple: $0 + 0$ to the complex: $$f(a) + \sum_{k=1}^{n} \frac{1}{k!} \frac{d^k}{dt^k}\bigg|_{t=0} f(u(t)) + \int_0^1 \frac{(1-t)^n}{n!} \frac{d^{n+1}}{dt^{n+1}} f(u(t))\, dt.$$ We can think of algebraic expressions as generalizations of common arithmetic operations that are formed by combining numbers, variables, and mathematical operations.
Myth and ritual	In traditional societies, Myth and ritual are two central components of religious practice. Although Myth and ritual are commonly united as parts of religion, the exact relationship between them has been a matter of controversy among scholars. One of the approaches to this problem is 'the Myth and ritual, or myth-ritualist, theory', which holds that 'myth does not stand by itself but is tied to ritual'.
Piety	In spiritual terminology, piety is a virtue that can mean religious devotion, spirituality, or a combination of both. A common element in most conceptions of piety is humility. The word piety comes from the Latin word pietas, the noun form of the adjective pius (which means 'devout' or 'good').
Violence	Violence is defined by the World Health Organization as the intentional use of physical force or power, threatened or actual, against oneself, another person, or against a group or community, that either results in or has a high likelihood of resulting in injury, death, psychological harm, maldevelopment or deprivation. This definition associates intentionality with the committing of the act itself, irrespective of the outcome it produces. Globally, violence takes the lives of more than 1.5 million people annually: just over 50% due to suicide, some 35% due to homicide, and just over 12% as a direct result of war or some other form of conflict.
Hermes Trismegistus	MythologyHermes Trismegistus Â· Thoth Â· Poimandres HermeticaCorpus Hermeticum Â· Kybalion Three Parts of the Wisdom of the Whole UniverseAlchemy Â· Astrology Â· Theurgy Influence and Influences Hermetic MovementsRosicrucianism

8. The Final Questions of Soul, Salvation, and the End of All Things: The ...

141

CHAPTER HIGHLIGHTS & NOTES: KEY TERMS, PEOPLE, PLACES, CONCEPTS

OrdersHermetic Order of the Golden Dawn Â· Hermetic Brotherhood of Luxor Â· Hermetic Brotherhood of Light

Topics in HermetismQabalah Occult and divinatory tarot Hermetists and HermeticistsJohn Dee . Aleister Crowley Â· Israel RegardieThÄbit ibn Qurra Â· ParacelsusGiordano Bruno Â· Manly P. Hall Â· Samuel MacGregor Mathers Â· William WestcottFranz BardonHermes Trismegistus is the representation of the combination of the Greek god Hermes and the Egyptian god Thoth. In Hellenistic Egypt, the Greeks recognised the congruence of their God Hermes with the Egyptian god Thoth.

Sharia	Sharia law is the moral code and religious law of Islam. Sharia deals with many topics addressed by secular law, including crime, politics and economics, as well as personal matters such as sexual intercourse, hygiene, diet, prayer, and fasting. Though interpretations of sharia vary between cultures, in its strictest definition it is considered the infallible law of God--as opposed to the human interpretation of the laws (fiqh).
Near-death experience	A near-death experience refers to a broad range of personal experiences associated with impending death, encompassing multiple possible sensations including detachment from the body; feelings of levitation; extreme fear; total serenity, security, or warmth; the experience of absolute dissolution; and the presence of a light. These phenomena are usually reported after an individual has been clinically dead or otherwise very close to death, hence the term near-death experience. Many NDE reports, however, originate from events that are not life-threatening.
Terrorism	Terrorism is the systematic use of terror, especially as a means of coercion. In the international community, however, terrorism has no universally agreed, legally binding, criminal law definition. Common definitions of terrorism refer only to those violent acts which are intended to create fear (terror), are perpetrated for a religious, political or, ideological goal; and deliberately target or disregard the safety of non-combatants (civilians).
Plato	Plato was a Classical Greek philosopher, mathematician, student of Socrates, writer of philosophical dialogues, and founder of the Academy in Athens, the first institution of higher learning in the Western world. Along with his mentor, Socrates, and his student, Aristotle, Plato helped to lay the foundations of Western philosophy and science. In the words of A. N. Whitehead:' The safest general characterization of the European philosophical tradition is that it consists of a series of footnotes to Plato.'
Republic	A republic is a state under a form of government in which the people, or some significant portion of them, retain supreme control over the government.

8. The Final Questions of Soul, Salvation, and the End of All Things: The ...

CHAPTER HIGHLIGHTS & NOTES: KEY TERMS, PEOPLE, PLACES, CONCEPTS

	The term is generally also understood to describe a state where most decisions are made with reference to established laws, rather than the discretion of a head of state, and therefore monarchy is today generally considered to be incompatible with being a republic. One common modern definition of a republic is a state without a monarch.
Padmasambhava	Padmasambhava Tibetan: ??????????????, Wylie: pad+ma 'byung gnas (EWTS), ZYPY: Bämajungnä); Mongolian ловон Бадмажунай, lovon Badmajunai, Chinese: ????? (pinyin: Liánhuasheng), Means The Lotus-Born, was a sage guru from Oddiyana who is said to have transmitted Vajrayana Buddhism to Bhutan and Tibet and neighboring countries in the 8th century.

In those lands he is better known as Guru Rinpoche ('Precious Guru') or Lopon Rinpoche, or, simply, Padum in Tibet, where followers of the Nyingma school regard him as the second Buddha.

He is further considered an emanation of Buddha Amitabha and traditionally even venerated as 'a second Buddha'. |
| Life After Life | Life After Life is a 1975 book written by psychiatrist Raymond Moody. It is a report on a qualitative study in which Moody interviewed 150 people who had undergone near-death experiences (NDEs). The book presents the author's composite account of what it is like to die. |
| Purity | Purity (suddha) is an important concept within much of Theravada and Mahayana Buddhism, although the implications of the resultant moral purification may be viewed differently in the varying traditions. The aim is to purify the personality of the Buddhist practitioner so that all moral and character defilements and defects (kleshas such as anger, ignorance and lust) are wiped away and Nirvana can be obtained.

Theravada Buddhism regards the path of self-purification as absolutely vital for the reaching of nibbana/nirvana. |
| Telepathy | Telepathy , is the ostensible transfer of information on thoughts or feelings between individuals by means other than the five senses. The term was coined in 1882 by the classical scholar Fredric W. H. Myers, a founder of the Society for Psychical Research, specifically to replace the earlier expression thought-transference. |
| Paranormal | Paranormal is a general term that describes unusual experiences that supposedly lack a scientific explanation, or phenomena alleged to be outside of science's current ability to explain or measure. Notably, Paranormal phenomena also lack scientific evidence, as detectable but not well explained phenomena such as dark matter or dark energy are not commonly called Paranormal.

In parapsychology, the term has, in the past, been used to describe the supposed phenomena of extra-sensory perception, including telepathy, and psychokinesis, ghosts, and hauntings. |

8. The Final Questions of Soul, Salvation, and the End of All Things: The ...

143

Embraced by the Light	Embraced by the Light is a #1 New York Times bestselling book by Betty Eadie describing her near-death experience (NDE). Eadie's NDE lasted several hours, one of the longest ever. Her book is arguably the most detailed near-death account on record.
Exclusivism	Exclusivism is the practice of being exclusive; mentality characterized by the disregard for opinions and ideas other than one's own, or the practice of organizing entities into groups by excluding those entities which possess certain traits like Christopher Columbus.. Religious exclusivism asserts that one religion is true and that all others are in error. It has two forms:•Absolute exclusivism asserts that one must be born into the religion to be a true adherent.
History of religions	The history of religion refers to the written record of human religious experiences and ideas. This period of religious history begins with the invention of writing about 5,000 years ago (3,000 BCE) in the Near East. The prehistory of religion relates to a study of religious beliefs that existed prior to the advent of written records. The timeline of religion is a comparative chronology of religion. The word 'religion' as it is used today does not have an obvious pre-colonial translation into non-European languages. Daniel Dubuisson writes that 'what the West and the history of religions in its wake have objectified under the name 'religion' is ... something quite unique, which could be appropriate only to itself and its own history.' The history of other cultures' interaction with the religious category is therefore their interaction with an idea that first developed in Europe under the influence of Christianity.
Stoicism	Stoicism is a school of Hellenistic philosophy founded in Athens by Zeno of Citium in the early 3rd century BC. The Stoics taught that destructive emotions resulted from errors in judgment, and that a sage, or person of 'moral and intellectual perfection,' would not suffer such emotions. Stoics were concerned with the active relationship between cosmic determinism and human freedom, and the belief that it is virtuous to maintain a will (called prohairesis) that is in accord with nature.
Reflexivity	Reflexivity refers to circular relationships between cause and effect. A reflexive relationship is bidirectional with both the cause and the effect affecting one another in a situation that does not render both functions causes and effects. In sociology, reflexivity therefore comes to mean an act of self-reference where examination or action 'bends back on', refers to, and affects the entity instigating the action or examination.
Akbar	Jalaluddin Muhammad Akbar also known as Akbar the Great (October 15, 1542 - October 27, 1605) was the third Mughal Emperor of India. He was of Turko-Mongol Timurid descent.; the son of Humayun, and the grandson of Babur who founded the dynasty.

8. The Final Questions of Soul, Salvation, and the End of All Things: The ...

CHAPTER HIGHLIGHTS & NOTES: KEY TERMS, PEOPLE, PLACES, CONCEPTS

Voltaire	François-Marie Arouet, was a French Enlightenment writer, historian and philosopher famous for his wit and for his advocacy of civil liberties, including freedom of religion, freedom of expression, free trade and separation of church and state. Voltaire was a prolific writer, producing works in almost every literary form, including plays, poetry, novels, essays, and historical and scientific works. He wrote more than 20,000 letters and more than 2,000 books and pamphlets.
Ralph Waldo Emerson	Ralph Waldo Emerson was an American essayist, lecturer, and poet, who led the Transcendentalist movement of the mid-19th century. He was seen as a champion of individualism and a prescient critic of the countervailing pressures of society, and he disseminated his thoughts through dozens of published essays and more than 1,500 public lectures across the United States. Emerson gradually moved away from the religious and social beliefs of his contemporaries, formulating and expressing the philosophy of Transcendentalism in his 1836 essay, Nature.
Authority	Authority is the legitimate or socially approved use of power. It is the legitimate power which one person or a group holds over another. The element of legitimacy is vital to the notion of authority and is the main means by which authority is distinguished from the more general concept of power.
Perception	Perception is the organization, identification, and interpretation of sensory information in order to fabricate a mental representation through the process of transduction, which sensors in the body transform signals from the environment into encoded neural signals. All perception involves signals in the nervous system, which in turn result from physical stimulation of the sense organs. For example, vision involves light striking the retinas of the eyes, smell is mediated by odor molecules and hearing involves pressure waves.
Apologetics	Apologetics is the discipline of defending a position (often religious) through the systematic use of information. Early Christian writers (c. 120-220) who defended their faith against critics and recommended their faith to outsiders were called apologists. The term apologetics etymologically derives from the Classical Greek word apologia.
Polemic	A polemic is a contentious argument that is intended to establish the truth of a specific belief and the falsity of the contrary belief. Polemics are mostly seen in arguments about very controversial topics. The art or practice of such argumentation is called polemics.
Creation myth	A creation myth is a symbolic narrative of a culture, tradition or people that describes their earliest beginnings, how the world they know began and how they first came into it. Creation myths develop in oral traditions, and are the most common form of myth, found throughout human culture.

Universality	In statistical mechanics, universality is the observation that there are properties for a large class of systems that are independent of the dynamical details of the system. Systems display universality in a scaling limit, when a large number of interacting parts come together. The modern meaning of the term was introduced by Leo Kadanoff in the 1960s, but a simpler version of the concept was already implicit in the van der Waals equation and in the earlier Landau theory of phase transitions, which did not incorporate scaling correctly.
Inclusivism	Inclusivism, one of several approaches to understanding the relationship between religions, asserts that while one set of beliefs is absolutely true, other sets of beliefs are at least partially true. It stands in contrast to exclusivism, which asserts that only one way is true and all others are in error. It is a particular form of religious pluralism, though that term may also assert that all beliefs are equally valid within a believer's particular context.
Contextualism	Contextualism describes a collection of views in philosophy which emphasize the context in which an action, utterance, or expression occurs, and argues that, in some important respect, the action, utterance, or expression can only be understood relative to that context. Contextualist views hold that philosophically controversial concepts, such as 'meaning P,' 'knowing that P,' 'having a reason to A,' and possibly even 'being true' or 'being right' only have meaning relative to a specified context. Some philosophers hold that context-dependence may lead to relativism; nevertheless, contextualist views are increasingly popular within philosophy.
Conversion	Conversion is a concept in traditional logic referring to a 'type of immediate inference in which from a given proposition, another proposition is inferred which has as its subject the predicate of the original proposition and as its predicate the subject of the original proposition (the quality of the proposition being retained)'. The immediately inferred proposition is termed the converse of the original proposition. Conversion has distinctive applications in philosophical logic and mathematical logic.
Damnation	Damnation is the concept of everlasting divine punishment and/or disgrace, especially the punishment for sin as threatened by God (e.g. Mark 3:29). A damned being 'in damnation' is said to be either in Hell, or living in a state wherein they are divorced from Heaven and/or in a state of disgrace from God's favor. Those Christians in purgatory, the 'Church Suffering', are not considered damned, because their stay there is not eternal, while people who are damned to Hell will stay there eternally.
Theory	In mathematical logic, a theory (also called a formal theory) is a set of sentences in a formal language. Usually a deductive system is understood from context. An element $\phi \in T$ of a theory T is then called an axiom of the theory, and any sentence that follows from the axioms ($T \vdash \phi$) is called a theorem of the theory.
Ernst Bergmann	Ernst Bergmann (7 August 1881, Colditz, Kingdom of Saxony - 16 April 1945, Naumburg) was a German philosopher and proponent of Nazism.

8. The Final Questions of Soul, Salvation, and the End of All Things: The ...

CHAPTER HIGHLIGHTS & NOTES: KEY TERMS, PEOPLE, PLACES, CONCEPTS

He studied philosophy and German philology at the University of Leipzig and got his PhD in 1905. Subsequently he continued his studies in Berlin. Later he returned to Leipzig, where he received the status of Privatdozent at the university in 1911. In 1916 he was awarded the position of Ausserordentlicher Professor (professor without chair).

Dilemma	A dilemma is a problem offering at least two possibilities, neither of which is practically acceptable. One in this position has been traditionally described as 'being on the horns of a dilemma', neither horn being comfortable, 'between Scylla and Charybdis'; or 'being between a rock and a hard place', since both objects or metaphorical choices are rough. This is sometimes more colorfully described as 'Finding oneself impaled upon the horns of a dilemma', referring to the sharp points of a bull's horns, equally uncomfortable (and dangerous).
Sociology	Sociology is the study of human social behavior and its origins, development, organizations, and institutions. It is a social science which uses various methods of empirical investigation and critical analysis to develop a body of knowledge about human social actions, social structure and functions. A goal for many sociologists is to conduct research which may be applied directly to social policy and welfare, while others focus primarily on refining the theoretical understanding of social processes.
Nostra Aetate	Nostra Aetate is the Declaration on the Relation of the Church with Non-Christian Religions of the Second Vatican Council. Passed by a vote of 2,221 to 88 of the assembled bishops, this declaration was promulgated on October 28, 1965, by Pope Paul VI. The first draft, entitled 'Decree on the Jews' , was completed in November 1961, approximately fourteen months after Cardinal Bea was commissioned by Pope John XXIII. This draft essentially went nowhere, never having been submitted to the Council, which opened on 11 October 1962. · Introduction · Hindus, Buddhists, and other religions · Muslims · Jews · Conclusion · The Declaration begins by describing the unity of the origin of all people, and the fact that they all return to God; hence their final goal is also one.
Quran	The Quran, also transliterated Qur'an, Koran, Al-Coran, Coran, Kuran, and Al-Qur'an, is the central religious text of Islam, which Muslims consider the verbatim word of God . It is regarded widely as the finest piece of literature in the Arabic language. The Quran is composed of verses (Ayah) that make up 114 chapters (suras) of unequal length which are classified either as Meccan or Medinan depending upon the place and time of their claimed revelation.

8. The Final Questions of Soul, Salvation, and the End of All Things: The ...

147

Buddha	Usually Buddha refers to SiddhÄrtha Gautama , the historical founder of Buddhism, for this Buddha age, who adopted that title. He is sometimes referred to as Sakyamuni or The Buddha Gautama , in order to distinguish him from other Buddha s (cf. Buddha hood, enlightenment, nirvana.)
Vishnu	Vishnu is the Supreme God in the Vaishnavite tradition of Hinduism. Smarta followers of Adi Shankara, among others, venerate Vishnu as one of the five primary forms of God. He is exalted as the highest God in Hindu sacred texts like the Taittiriya Samhita and the Bhagavad Gita.
Caste	A caste is a combined social system of occupation, endogamy, culture, social class, and political power. caste should not be confused with class, in that members of a caste are deemed to be alike in function or culture, whereas not all members of a defined class may be so alike. Although Indian society is often now associated with the word 'caste', it was first used by the Portuguese to describe inherited class status in their own European society.
Spiritual But Not Religious	Spiritual But Not Religious is a popular phrase and acronym used to self-identify a life stance of spirituality that rejects traditional organized religion as the sole or most valuable means of furthering spiritual growth. The term is used world-wide, but seems most prominent in the United States where one study reports that as many as 33% of people identify as spiritual but not religious. Other surveys report lower percentages ranging from 24%-10% Those that identify as SBNR vary in their individual spiritual philosophies and practices and theological references.
World Religions	World Religions was an educational television show which was produced and broadcast by TVOntario (known at the time as the Ontario Educational Communications Authority) in 1973. The three episode names known are:•'Judaism'•'Who Do Men Say That I Am?'•'Islam: Terrorists or Visionaries' All episodes were 30 minutes in length.
EPIC	EPIC (Executive-Process/Interactive Control) is a cognitive architecture developed by Professors David E. Kieras and David E. Meyer at the University of Michigan . EPIC has components that emulate various parts of the human-information processing system. Among these components are tools for perceptual, cognitive, and motor processing.
Civil Rights	Civil and political rights are a class of rights that protect individuals' freedom from unwarranted infringement by governments and private organizations, and ensure one's ability to participate in the civil and political life of the state without discrimination or repression.

8. The Final Questions of Soul, Salvation, and the End of All Things: The ...

CHAPTER HIGHLIGHTS & NOTES: KEY TERMS, PEOPLE, PLACES, CONCEPTS

Civil rights include the ensuring of peoples' physical and mental integrity, life and safety; protection from discrimination on grounds such as race, gender, sexual orientation, gender identity, national origin, colour, ethnicity, religion, or disability; and individual rights such as privacy, the freedoms of thought and conscience, speech and expression, religion, the press, assembly and movement.

Political rights include natural justice in law, such as the rights of the accused, including the right to a fair trial; due process; the right to seek redress or a legal remedy; and rights of participation in civil society and politics such as freedom of association, the right to assemble, the right to petition, the right of self-defense, and the right to vote.

Equality	Loosely, equality is the state of being quantitatively the same. More formally, equality is the binary relation on a set X defined by $\{(x,x) \mid x \in X\}$.

The identity relation is the archetype of the more general concept of an equivalence relation on a set: those binary relations which are reflexive, symmetric, and transitive. The relation of equality is also antisymmetric.

Justice

Justice is a concept of moral rightness based on ethics, rationality, law, natural law, religion, or equity. It is also the act of being just and/or fair.

According to most contemporary theories of justice, justice is overwhelmingly important: John Rawls claims that 'Justice is the first virtue of social institutions, as truth is of systems of thought.' Justice can be thought of as distinct from and more fundamental than benevolence, charity, mercy, generosity, or compassion.

Liberation theology

Liberation theology is a political movement in Christian theology which interprets the teachings of Jesus Christ in terms of a liberation from unjust economic, political, or social conditions. It has been described by proponents as 'an interpretation of Christian faith through the poor's suffering, their struggle and hope, and a critique of society and the Catholic faith and Christianity through the eyes of the poor', and by detractors as Christianized Marxism.

Although liberation theology has grown into an international and inter-denominational movement, it began as a movement within the Roman Catholic church in Latin America in the 1950s-1960s.

Social justice

Social justice generally refers to the idea of creating a society or institution that is based on the principles of equality and solidarity, that understands and values human rights, and that recognizes the dignity of every human being.

Social justice is based on the concepts of human rights and equality and involves a greater degree of economic egalitarianism through progressive taxation, income redistribution, or even property redistribution.

8. The Final Questions of Soul, Salvation, and the End of All Things: The ...

149

Criticism	Criticism is the practice of judging the merits and faults of something or someone in an intelligible (or articulate) way. •The judger is called 'the critic'.•To engage in criticism is 'to criticize'.•One specific item of criticism is called 'a criticism'.
	Criticism can be:•directed toward a person or an animal; at a group, authority or organization; at a specific behaviour; or at an object of some kind (an idea, a relationship, a condition, a process, or a thing).•personal (delivered directly from one person to another, in a personal capacity), or impersonal (expressing the view of an organization, and not aimed at anyone personally).•highly specific and detailed, or very abstract and general.•verbal (expressed in language) or non-verbal (expressed symbolically, or expressed through an action or a way of behaving).•explicit (the criticism is clearly stated) or implicit (a criticism is implied by what is being said, but it is not stated openly).•the result of critical thinking or spontaneous impulse.
	To criticize does not necessarily imply 'to find fault', but the word is often taken to mean the simple expression of an objection against prejudice, or a disapproval. Often criticism involves active disagreement, but it may only mean 'taking sides'.
Historical criticism	
	Historical criticism, is a branch of literary criticism that investigates the origins of ancient text in order to understand 'the world behind the text'.
	The primary goal of historical criticism is to ascertain the text's primitive or original meaning in its original historical context and its literal sense or sensus literalis historicus. The secondary goal seeks to establish a reconstruction of the historical situation of the author and recipients of the text.
Black theology	Black theology refers to a variety of Black theologies which has as its base in the liberation of the marginalized, especially the injustice done towards blacks in American and South African contexts. Black theology mixes liberation theology and the work of Paulo Freire with the civil rights and black power movements.
	Black theology is a form of liberation theology that has its center in the theme of oppression of black people by white people.
Patriarchy	Patriarchy is a social system in which the role of the male as the primary authority figure is central to social organization, and where fathers hold authority over women, children, and property. It implies the institutions of male rule and privilege, and is dependent on female subordination.
	Historically, the principle of patriarchy has been central to the social, legal, political, and economic organization of Celtic, Germanic, Roman, Greek, Hebrew, Arabian, Indian, and Chinese cultures, and has had a deep influence on modern civilization.

8. The Final Questions of Soul, Salvation, and the End of All Things: The ...

CHAPTER HIGHLIGHTS & NOTES: KEY TERMS, PEOPLE, PLACES, CONCEPTS

Feminist theology	Feminist theology is a movement found in several religions, including Buddhism, Christianity, Judaism, and New Thought, to reconsider the traditions, practices, scriptures, and theologies of those religions from a feminist perspective. Some of the goals of feminist theology include increasing the role of women among the clergy and religious authorities, reinterpreting male-dominated imagery and language about God, determining women's place in relation to career and motherhood, and studying images of women in the religion's sacred texts and matriarchal religion. Feminist theology attempts to consider every aspect of religious practice and thought.
Suffrage	Suffrage, political franchise, or simply the franchise is the civil right to vote, or the exercise of that right. In English, suffrage and its synonyms are sometimes also used to mean the right to run for office (to be a candidate), but there are no established qualifying terms to distinguish between these different meanings of the term(s). The right to run for office is sometimes called (candidate) eligibility, and the combination of both rights is sometimes called full suffrage.
Queer theology	Queer Theology is concerned with religious questions about the meaning of existence, as they are posed by lesbian, gay, transgender, intersex, bisexual, or in some other way queer seekers. The classic problems of theology apply: the problems of both natural and human evil; the problem of God or the ultimate source of the universe; the problem of the purpose of human life; the problem of ethical conduct; and the problem of human desire for eternal life. Queer Theology is distinct from theology, because the teleological significance of same-sex love remains a mystery, and because the orthodox theologies of the most powerful religions have traditionally been used as weapons against sexual minorities.
Womanist theology	Womanist theology is a religious conceptual framework which reconsiders and revises the traditions, practices, scriptures, and biblical interpretation with a special lens to empower and liberate African American women in America. Womanist theology associates with and departs from Feminist theology and Black theology specifically because it integrates the perspectives and experiences of African American and other women of color. The former's lack of attention to the everyday realities of women of color and the latter's lack of understanding of the full dimension of liberation from the unique oppressions of Black women require bringing them together in Womanist Theology. The goals of womanist theology include interrogating the social construction of black womanhood in relation to the Black community and to assume a liberatory perspective so that African American women can live emboldened lives within the African American community and within the larger society.
Judith Butler	Judith Butler is an American post-structuralist philosopher, who has contributed to the fields of feminism, queer theory, political philosophy, and ethics. She is a professor in the Rhetoric and Comparative Literature departments at the University of California, Berkeley. Butler received her PhD in philosophy from Yale University in 1984, for a dissertation subsequently published as Subjects of Desire: Hegelian Reflections in Twentieth-Century France.

8. The Final Questions of Soul, Salvation, and the End of All Things: The ...

151

CHAPTER HIGHLIGHTS & NOTES: KEY TERMS, PEOPLE, PLACES, CONCEPTS

Homosexuality	Homosexuality is romantic attraction, sexual attraction or sexual behavior between members of the same sex or gender. As an orientation, homosexuality refers to 'an enduring pattern of or disposition to experience sexual, affectionate, or romantic attractions' primarily or exclusively to people of the same sex. 'It also refers to an individual's sense of personal and social identity based on those attractions, behaviors expressing them, and membership in a community of others who share them.' Along with bisexuality and heterosexuality, homosexuality is one of the three main categories of sexual orientation within the heterosexual-homosexual continuum.
Celibacy	Celibacy refers to a state of being unmarried, or a state of abstinence from sexual intercourse or the abstention by vow from marriage. The English word celibacy derives from the Latin caelibatus, 'state of being unmarried', from Latin caelebs, meaning 'unmarried'. This word derives from two Proto-Indo-European stems, *kaiwelo- 'alone' and *lib(h)s- 'living'.
Ambedkar	Bhimrao Ramji Ambedkar (14 April 1891 -- 6 December 1956), also known as Babasaheb, was an Indian jurist, political leader, Buddhist activist, philosopher, thinker, anthropologist, historian, orator, prolific writer, economist, scholar, editor, revolutionary and the revivalist of Buddhism in India. He was also the chief architect of the Indian Constitution. Born into a poor Mahar so called Untouchable family, Ambedkar spent his whole life fighting against social discrimination, the system of Chaturvarna -- the Hindu categorization of human society into four varnas -- and the Hindu caste system.
Dalit	Dalit, is a self-designation for a group of people traditionally regarded as of Untouchables and unsuitable for making personal relationships. Dalits are a mixed population of numerous caste groups all over South Asia, and speak various languages. While the caste system has been abolished under the Indian constitution, there is still discrimination and prejudice against Dalits in South Asia.

8. The Final Questions of Soul, Salvation, and the End of All Things: The ...

1. A _____ is a state under a form of government in which the people, or some significant portion of them, retain supreme control over the government. The term is generally also understood to describe a state where most decisions are made with reference to established laws, rather than the discretion of a head of state, and therefore monarchy is today generally considered to be incompatible with being a _____. One common modern definition of a _____ is a state without a monarch.

   a. Bagar
   b. Republic
   c. Commentaries on Plato
   d. Dianoia

2. In philosophy, _____ is the view that all matter has a mental aspect, or, alternatively, all objects have a unified center of experience or point of view. Baruch Spinoza, Gottfried Leibniz, Gustav Theodor Fechner, Friedrich Paulsen, Ernst Haeckel, Charles Strong, and partially William James are considered panpsychists.

   Panexperientialism, as espoused by Alfred North Whitehead, is a less bold variation, which credits all entities with phenomenal consciousness but not with cognition, and therefore not necessarily with full-fledged minds.

   a. Phenomenalism
   b. Panpsychism
   c. Property dualism
   d. Psychological egoism

3. _____ is a general term for techniques typically used by philosophers in the analytic tradition that involve 'breaking down' (i.e. analyzing) philosophical issues.

   a. Racing thoughts
   b. Synectics
   c. The British Society for the Philosophy of Religion
   d. Philosophical analysis

4. _____ is, in a broad sense, the rejection of belief in the existence of deities. In a narrower sense, _____ is specifically the position that there are no deities. Most inclusively, _____ is simply the absence of belief that any deities exist.

   a. Eroakirkosta.fi
   b. Infidel
   c. Adriaan Koerbagh
   d. Atheism

5. . _____ is the legitimate or socially approved use of power. It is the legitimate power which one person or a group holds over another. The element of legitimacy is vital to the notion of _____ and is the main means by which _____ is distinguished from the more general concept of power.

8. The Final Questions of Soul, Salvation, and the End of All Things: The ...

153

a. EQuibbly

b. European Association of Social Psychology

c. Evasion

d. Authority

1. b
2. b
3. d
4. d
5. d

You can take the complete Chapter Practice Test

for 8. The Final Questions of Soul, Salvation, and the End of All Things: The ...

on all key terms, persons, places, and concepts.

Online 99 Cents

http://www.JustTheFacts101.com

Use www.JustTheFacts101.com for all your study needs

including Facts101's online interactive problem solving labs in

chemistry, statistics, mathematics, and more.

	Friedrich
	Nietzsche
	Rationalism
	Theodicy
	Agnosticism
	Reductionism
	Ernst Bergmann
	Psychology
	Representation
	Psychoanalysis
	Censorship
	Religious experience
	Oedipus complex
	Patriarchy
	Buddhism
	Mysticism
	Philosophical analysis
	Renaissance
	Libido
	Myth and ritual
	Primal scene

Sublimation

Belief

Sociology

Totem

Society

Knowledge society

Sociology of knowledge

Externalization

Objectification

History of religions

Orientalism

Darwinism

Contextualism

Conversion

Theory

Sufi

Stephen Jay Gould

Soul

Metaphor

Altruism

Near-death experience

CHAPTER OUTLINE: KEY TERMS, PEOPLE, PLACES, CONCEPTS

	Paranormal
	Reincarnation
	Sharia
	Expression
	Piety
	Suicide
	Terrorism
	Violence
	Coercive persuasion
	Deprogramming
	Sect
	Prophet
	Attitude
	Eschatology
	Atheism
	Liberalism

9. Faithful Re-readings: Exclusivism, Inclusivism, Pluralism, and Justice ...

Friedrich	The Friedrich are the most ancient German-Bohemian glass-maker family.
	History
	From as early as 750 years ago, the shadowy picture of the oldest German-Bohemian glass-maker family Friedrich emerges, who contributed greatly towards the creation of the world-famous Bohemian glass (also called Bohemian Crystal). In pre-Hussite times they produced amazing works of vitreous art near Daubitz, nowadays called Doubice.
Nietzsche	Friedrich Wilhelm Nietzsche was a 19th-century German philosopher and classical philologist. He wrote critical texts on religion, morality, contemporary culture, philosophy and science, using a distinctive German-language style and displaying a fondness for metaphor, irony and aphorism.
	Nietzsche's influence remains substantial within and beyond philosophy, notably in existentialism and postmodernism.
Rationalism	Rationalism in politics is often seen as the midpoint in the three major political viewpoints of realism, rationalism, and internationalism. Whereas Realism and Internationalism are both on ends of the scale, rationalism tends to occupy the middle ground on most issues, and finds compromise between these two conflicting points of view.
	Believers of Rationalism believe that multinational and multilateral organizations have their place in the world order, but not that a world government would be feasible.
Theodicy	The term theodicy has no universally agreed upon definition, but usually refers to an attempt to resolve the evidential problem of evil by reconciling God's traditional characteristics of omnibenevolence, omnipotence and omniscience (all-loving, all-powerful, and all-knowing, respectively) with the occurrence of evil in the world. Although some arguments existed previously, the term 'theodicy' was coined in 1710 by German philosopher Gottfried Leibniz in his work, Théodicée.
	A variety of theodicies exist.
Agnosticism	Agnosticism is the view that the truth values of certain claims--especially claims about the existence or non-existence of any deity, but also other religious and metaphysical claims--are unknown or unknowable. Agnosticism can be defined in various ways, and is sometimes used to indicate doubt or a skeptical approach to questions. In some senses, agnosticism is a stance about the difference between belief and knowledge, rather than about any specific claim or belief.

Reductionism	Reductionism can mean either (a) an approach to understanding the nature of complex things by reducing them to the interactions of their parts, or to simpler or more fundamental things or (b) a philosophical position that a complex system is nothing but the sum of its parts, and that an account of it can be reduced to accounts of individual constituents. This can be said of objects, phenomena, explanations, theories, and meanings. Reductionism strongly reflects a certain perspective on causality.
Ernst Bergmann	Ernst Bergmann (7 August 1881, Colditz, Kingdom of Saxony - 16 April 1945, Naumburg) was a German philosopher and proponent of Nazism. He studied philosophy and German philology at the University of Leipzig and got his PhD in 1905. Subsequently he continued his studies in Berlin. Later he returned to Leipzig, where he received the status of Privatdozent at the university in 1911. In 1916 he was awarded the position of Ausserordentlicher Professor (professor without chair).
Psychology	Psychology is an academic and applied discipline that involves the scientific study of mental functions and behaviors. Psychology has the immediate goal of understanding individuals and groups by both establishing general principles and researching specific cases, and by many accounts it ultimately aims to benefit society. In this field, a professional practitioner or researcher is called a psychologist and can be classified as a social, behavioral, or cognitive scientist.
Representation	Representation is the use of signs that stand in for and take the place of something else. It is through representation that people organize the world and reality through the act of naming its elements. Signs are arranged in order to form semantic constructions and express relations.
Psychoanalysis	Psychoanalysis is a body of ideas developed by Austrian neurologist Sigmund Freud and continued by others. It is primarily devoted to the study of human psychological functioning and behavior, although it can also be applied to societies. Psychoanalysis has three main components:•a method of investigation of the mind and the way one thinks;•a systematized set of theories about human behavior;•a method of treatment of psychological or emotional illness. Under the broad umbrella of psychoanalysis, there are at least 22 theoretical orientations regarding human mentation and development.
Censorship	Censorship is suppression of speech or other communication which may be considered objectionable, harmful, sensitive, or inconvenient to the general body of people as determined by a government, media outlet, or other controlling body. Rationale

	The rationale for censorship is different for various types of information censored:•Moral censorship is the removal of materials that are obscene or otherwise considered morally questionable. Pornography, for example, is often censored under this rationale, especially child pornography, which is illegal and censored in many jurisdictions in the world.•Military censorship is the process of keeping military intelligence and tactics confidential and away from the enemy.
Religious experience	A religious experience is a subjective experience in which an individual reports contact with a transcendent reality, an encounter or union with the divine. Such an experience often involves arriving at some knowledge or insight previously unavailable to the subject yet unaccountable or unforseeable according to the usual conceptual or psychological framework within which the subject has been used to operating. Religious experience generally brings understanding, partial or complete, of issues of a fundamental character that may have been a cause (whether consciously ackowledged or not) of anguish or alienation to the subject for an extended period of time.
Oedipus complex	In psychoanalytic theory, the term Oedipus complex denotes the emotions and ideas that the mind keeps in the unconscious, via dynamic repression, that concentrate upon a boy's desire to sexually possess his mother, and kill his father. In the course of his psychosexual development, the complex is the boy's phallic stage formation of a discrete sexual identity; a girl's analogous experience is the Electra complex. The Oedipus complex occurs in the third -- phallic stage (ages 3 -6) -- of five psychosexual development stages: (i) the Oral, (ii) the Anal, (iii) the Phallic, (iv) the Latent, and (v) the Genital -- in which the source libido pleasure is in a different erogenous zone of the infant's body.
Patriarchy	Patriarchy is a social system in which the role of the male as the primary authority figure is central to social organization, and where fathers hold authority over women, children, and property. It implies the institutions of male rule and privilege, and is dependent on female subordination. Historically, the principle of patriarchy has been central to the social, legal, political, and economic organization of Celtic, Germanic, Roman, Greek, Hebrew, Arabian, Indian, and Chinese cultures, and has had a deep influence on modern civilization.
Buddhism	Buddhism is a religion and philosophy indigenous to the Indian subcontinent that encompasses a variety of traditions, beliefs, and practices largely based on teachings attributed to Siddhartha Gautama, who is commonly known as the Buddha . The Buddha lived and taught in the eastern part of Indian subcontinent some time between the 6th and 4th centuries BCE. He is recognized by Buddhists as an awakened or enlightened teacher who shared his insights to help sentient beings end suffering (dukkha) through eliminating ignorance (avidya), craving , and hatred, by way of understanding and seeing dependent origination (pratityasamutpada) and non-self (anatman), and thus attain the highest happiness, nirvana (nirvana).

Mysticism	Mysticism is the pursuit of communion with, identity with divinity, spiritual truth intuition, instinct or insight. Mysticism usually centers on a practice or practices intended to nurture those experiences or awareness. Mysticism may be dualistic, maintaining a distinction between the self and the divine, or may be nondualistic.
Philosophical analysis	Philosophical analysis is a general term for techniques typically used by philosophers in the analytic tradition that involve 'breaking down' (i.e. analyzing) philosophical issues.
Renaissance	The Renaissance was a cultural movement that spanned the period roughly from the 14th to the 17th century, beginning in Italy in the Late Middle Ages and later spreading to the rest of Europe. Though the invention of printing sped the dissemination of ideas from the later 15th century, the changes of the Renaissance were not uniformly experienced across Europe. As a cultural movement, it encompassed innovative flowering of Latin and vernacular literatures, beginning with the 14th-century resurgence of learning based on classical sources, which contemporaries credited to Petrarch, the development of linear perspective and other techniques of rendering a more natural reality in painting, and gradual but widespread educational reform.
Libido	Libido refers to a person's sex drive or desire for sexual activity. The desire for sex is an aspect of a person's sexuality, but varies enormously from one person to another, and it also varies depending on circumstances at a particular time. Sex drive has usually biological, psychological, and social components.
Myth and ritual	In traditional societies, Myth and ritual are two central components of religious practice. Although Myth and ritual are commonly united as parts of religion, the exact relationship between them has been a matter of controversy among scholars. One of the approaches to this problem is 'the Myth and ritual, or myth-ritualist, theory', which holds that 'myth does not stand by itself but is tied to ritual'.
Primal scene	In psychoanalysis, the primal scene is the initial witnessing by a child of a sex act, usually between the parents, that traumatizes the psychosexual development of that child. The scene witnessed may also occur between animals, and be displaced onto humans. Ned Lukacher has proposed using the term in literary criticism to refer to a kind of intertextuality in which the ability to interpret one text depends on the meaning of another text.
Sublimation	In psychology, sublimation is a term coined by Freud which was eventually used to describe the spirit as a reflection of the libido. It has its roots in Freud's psychoanalytical approach, and is sometimes also referred to as a type of defense mechanism. According to Wade and Tavris, sublimation is when displacement 'serves a higher cultural or socially useful purpose, as in the creation of art or inventions.' Psychoanalytic theory

9. Faithful Re-readings: Exclusivism, Inclusivism, Pluralism, and Justice ...

Belief	Belief is the psychological state in which an individual holds a proposition or premise to be true.
	The terms belief and knowledge are used differently in philosophy.
	Epistemology is the philosophical study of knowledge and belief.
Sociology	Sociology is the study of human social behavior and its origins, development, organizations, and institutions. It is a social science which uses various methods of empirical investigation and critical analysis to develop a body of knowledge about human social actions, social structure and functions. A goal for many sociologists is to conduct research which may be applied directly to social policy and welfare, while others focus primarily on refining the theoretical understanding of social processes.
Totem	A Totem is any supposed entity that watches over or assists a group of people, such as a family, clan, or tribe.
	Totems support larger groups than the individual person. In kinship and descent, if the apical ancestor of a clan is nonhuman, it is called a Totem.
Society	A society, or a human society, is a group of people involved with each other through persistent relations, or a large social grouping sharing the same geographical or social territory, subject to the same political authority and dominant cultural expectations. Human societies are characterized by patterns of relationships (social relations) between individuals who share a distinctive culture and institutions; a given society may be described as the sum total of such relationships among its constituent members. In the social sciences, a larger society often evinces stratification and/or dominance patterns in subgroups.
Knowledge society	Broadly speaking, the term Knowledge society refers to any society where knowledge is the primary production resource instead of capital and labour. It may also refer to the use a certain society gives to information. A Knowledge society 'creates, shares and uses knowledge for the prosperity and well-being of its people'.
Sociology of knowledge	The Sociology of knowledge is the study of the relationship between human thought and the social context within which it arises, and of the effects prevailing ideas have on societies. It is not a specialized area of sociology but instead deals with broad fundamental questions about the extent and limits of social influences on individual's lives and the social-cultural basics of our knowledge about the world.
	The sociology of knowledge was pioneered primarily by the sociologists Émile Durkheim and Marcel Mauss at the end of the 19th and beginning of the 20th centuries.

Externalization	Externalization means to put something outside of its original borders, especially to put a human function outside of the human body. The opposite of externalization is internalization.
	In a concrete sense, by taking notes, we can externalize the function of memory which normally belongs in the brain.
Objectification	Objectification is the process by which an abstract concept is made as objective as possible in the purest sense of the term. It is also treated as if it is a concrete thing or physical object. In this sense the term is a synonym to reification.
History of religions	The history of religion refers to the written record of human religious experiences and ideas. This period of religious history begins with the invention of writing about 5,000 years ago (3,000 BCE) in the Near East. The prehistory of religion relates to a study of religious beliefs that existed prior to the advent of written records. The timeline of religion is a comparative chronology of religion.
	The word 'religion' as it is used today does not have an obvious pre-colonial translation into non-European languages. Daniel Dubuisson writes that 'what the West and the history of religions in its wake have objectified under the name 'religion' is ... something quite unique, which could be appropriate only to itself and its own history.' The history of other cultures' interaction with the religious category is therefore their interaction with an idea that first developed in Europe under the influence of Christianity.
Orientalism	Orientalism is a term used by art historians, literary and cultural studies scholars for the imitation or depiction of aspects of Middle Eastern, and East Asian cultures (Eastern cultures) by American and European writers, designers and artists. In particular, Orientalist painting, depicting more specifically 'the Middle East', was one of the many specialisms of 19th century Academic art. Since the publication of Edward Said's Orientalism, the term has arguably acquired a negative connotation.
Darwinism	Darwinism is a set of movements and concepts related to ideas of transmutation of species or evolution, including ideas with no connection to the work of Charles Darwin. The meaning of 'Darwinism' has changed over time, and varies depending on who is using the term. In the United States, the term 'Darwinism' is often used by creationists as a pejorative term, but in the United Kingdom the term has no negative connotations, being freely used as a short hand for evolutionary theory.
Contextualism	Contextualism describes a collection of views in philosophy which emphasize the context in which an action, utterance, or expression occurs, and argues that, in some important respect, the action, utterance, or expression can only be understood relative to that context. Contextualist views hold that philosophically controversial concepts, such as 'meaning P,' 'knowing that P,' 'having a reason to A,' and possibly even 'being true' or 'being right' only have meaning relative to a specified context.

9. Faithful Re-readings: Exclusivism, Inclusivism, Pluralism, and Justice ...

Conversion	Conversion is a concept in traditional logic referring to a 'type of immediate inference in which from a given proposition, another proposition is inferred which has as its subject the predicate of the original proposition and as its predicate the subject of the original proposition (the quality of the proposition being retained)'. The immediately inferred proposition is termed the converse of the original proposition. Conversion has distinctive applications in philosophical logic and mathematical logic.
Theory	In mathematical logic, a theory (also called a formal theory) is a set of sentences in a formal language. Usually a deductive system is understood from context. An element $\phi \in T$ of a theory T is then called an axiom of the theory, and any sentence that follows from the axioms ($T \vdash \phi$) is called a theorem of the theory.
Sufi	The lexical root of Sufi is variously traced to ØµÙÙˆÙ á¹£Å«f 'wool', referring either to the simple cloaks the early Muslim ascetics wore, or possibly to ØµÙŽÙØ§ á¹£afÄ 'purity'. The two were combined by al-Rudhabari who said, 'The Sufi is the one who wears wool on top of purity.' The wool cloaks were sometimes a designation of their initiation into the Sufi order. The early Sufi orders considered the wearing of this coat an imitation of Isa bin Maryam (Jesus).
Stephen Jay Gould	Stephen Jay Gould was an American paleontologist, evolutionary biologist and historian of science. He was also one of the most influential and widely read writers of popular science of his generation. Gould spent most of his career teaching at Harvard University and working at the American Museum of Natural History in New York.
Soul	The soul--in many traditional spiritual, philosophical, and psychological traditions--is the incorporeal and immortal essence of a person, living thing, or object. According to some religions (including the Abrahamic religions in most of their forms), souls--or at least immortal souls capable of union with the divine--belong only to human beings. For example, the Catholic theologian Thomas Aquinas attributed 'soul' (anima) to all organisms but taught that only human souls are immortal.
Metaphor	A metaphor is a literary figure of speech that describes a subject by asserting that it is, on some point of comparison, the same as another otherwise unrelated object. Metaphor is a type of analogy and is closely related to other rhetorical figures of speech that achieve their effects via association, comparison or resemblance including allegory, hyperbole, and simile. One of the most prominent examples of a metaphor in English literature is the All the world's a stage monologue from As You Like It:All the world's a stage,And all the men and women merely players;They have their exits and their entrances; -- William Shakespeare, As You Like It, 2/7 This quote is a metaphor because the world is not literally a stage.
Altruism	Altruism is a concern for the welfare of others.

It is a traditional virtue in many cultures, and a core aspect of various religious traditions, though the concept of 'others' toward whom concern should be directed can vary among cultures and religions. Altruism is the opposite of selfishness.

Near-death experience	A near-death experience refers to a broad range of personal experiences associated with impending death, encompassing multiple possible sensations including detachment from the body; feelings of levitation; extreme fear; total serenity, security, or warmth; the experience of absolute dissolution; and the presence of a light. These phenomena are usually reported after an individual has been clinically dead or otherwise very close to death, hence the term near-death experience. Many NDE reports, however, originate from events that are not life-threatening.
Paranormal	Paranormal is a general term that describes unusual experiences that supposedly lack a scientific explanation, or phenomena alleged to be outside of science's current ability to explain or measure. Notably, Paranormal phenomena also lack scientific evidence, as detectable but not well explained phenomena such as dark matter or dark energy are not commonly called Paranormal. In parapsychology, the term has, in the past, been used to describe the supposed phenomena of extra-sensory perception, including telepathy, and psychokinesis, ghosts, and hauntings.
Reincarnation	Reincarnation is a 2008 fantasy novel by American author Suzanne Weyn. The novel was released on January 1, 2008. It tells the story of a two lovers who attempt to find each other through the centuries. The narrative follows the action through time.
Sharia	Sharia law is the moral code and religious law of Islam. Sharia deals with many topics addressed by secular law, including crime, politics and economics, as well as personal matters such as sexual intercourse, hygiene, diet, prayer, and fasting. Though interpretations of sharia vary between cultures, in its strictest definition it is considered the infallible law of God--as opposed to the human interpretation of the laws (fiqh).
Expression	In mathematics, an expression is a finite combination of symbols that is well-formed according to rules that depend on the context. Symbols can designate numbers (constants), variables, operations, functions, and other mathematical symbols, as well as punctuation, symbols of grouping, and other syntactic symbols. The use of expressions can range from the simple: $0 + 0$

to the complex:

$$f(a) + \sum_{k=1}^{n} \frac{1}{k!} \frac{d^k}{dt^k}\bigg|_{t=0} f(u(t)) + \int_0^1 \frac{(1-t)^n}{n!} \frac{d^{n+1}}{dt^{n+1}} f(u(t))\, dt.$$

9. Faithful Re-readings: Exclusivism, Inclusivism, Pluralism, and Justice ...

Piety	In spiritual terminology, piety is a virtue that can mean religious devotion, spirituality, or a combination of both. A common element in most conceptions of piety is humility. The word piety comes from the Latin word pietas, the noun form of the adjective pius (which means 'devout' or 'good').
Suicide	Suicide is the act of intentionally causing one's own death. Suicide is often committed out of despair, the cause of which is frequently attributed to a mental disorder such as depression, bipolar disorder, schizophrenia, alcoholism, or drug abuse. Stress factors such as financial difficulties or troubles with interpersonal relationships often play a role.
Terrorism	Terrorism is the systematic use of terror, especially as a means of coercion. In the international community, however, terrorism has no universally agreed, legally binding, criminal law definition. Common definitions of terrorism refer only to those violent acts which are intended to create fear (terror), are perpetrated for a religious, political or, ideological goal; and deliberately target or disregard the safety of non-combatants (civilians).
Violence	Violence is defined by the World Health Organization as the intentional use of physical force or power, threatened or actual, against oneself, another person, or against a group or community, that either results in or has a high likelihood of resulting in injury, death, psychological harm, maldevelopment or deprivation. This definition associates intentionality with the committing of the act itself, irrespective of the outcome it produces. Globally, violence takes the lives of more than 1.5 million people annually: just over 50% due to suicide, some 35% due to homicide, and just over 12% as a direct result of war or some other form of conflict.
Coercive persuasion	Coercive persuasion comprises social influences capable of producing substantial changes in behavior, attitude, and ideology through the use of coercive tactics and persuasion, via interpersonal and group-based influences. The term was coined by Edgar Schein in 1961 in relation to his study of Chinese POWs' indoctrination. According to Schein, the essence of coercive persuasion, .. is to produce ideological and behavioral changes in a fully conscious, mentally intact individual.
Deprogramming	Deprogramming is an attempt to force a person to abandon allegiance to a religious, political, economic, or social group. Methods and practices may involve kidnapping and coercion. The person in question is taken against his/her will, which has led to controversies over freedom of religion, kidnapping and civil rights, as well as the violence which is sometimes involved.

Sect	Sect is an ancient astrological concept in which the seven traditional 'planets' (including the Sun, the Moon and the five starry planets) are assigned to two different categories: diurnal or nocturnal Sect.
	Diurnal planets are more comfortable and powerful when they appear in charts in which the Sun is above the horizon. They include:
	· Sun · Jupiter · Saturn
	Nocturnal planets are more comfortable and powerful when they appear in charts in which the Sun is below the horizon, or at night.
Prophet	In religion, a prophet is an individual who is claimed to have been contacted by the supernatural or the divine, and to speak for them, serving as an intermediary with humanity, delivering this newfound knowledge from the supernatural entity to other people. The message that the prophet conveys is called a prophecy.
	Claims of prophets have existed in many cultures through history, including Judaism, Christianity, Islam, the Sybilline and the Pythia, known as the Oracle of Delphi, in Ancient Greece, Zoroaster, the Völuspá in Old Norse and many others.
Attitude	Attitude as a term of fine art refers to the posture or gesture given to a figure by a painter or sculptor. It applies to the body and not to a mental state, but the arrangement of the body is presumed to serve a communicative or expressive purpose. An example of a conventional attitude in art is proskynesis to indicate respect toward God, emperors, clerics of high status, and religious icons; in Byzantine art, it is particularly characteristic in depictions of the emperor paying homage to Christ.
Eschatology	Eschatology is a part of theology, philosophy, and futurology concerned with what are believed to be the final events of history, the ultimate destiny of humanity--commonly referred to as the 'end of the world' or 'end time'.
	The Oxford English Dictionary defines eschatology as 'The department of theological science concerned with 'the four last things: death, judgement, heaven, and hell'.'
	In the context of mysticism, the phrase refers metaphorically to the end of ordinary reality and reunion with the Divine. In many religions it is taught as an existing future event prophesied in sacred texts or folklore.
Atheism	Atheism is, in a broad sense, the rejection of belief in the existence of deities. In a narrower sense, atheism is specifically the position that there are no deities.

9. Faithful Re-readings: Exclusivism, Inclusivism, Pluralism, and Justice ...

| Liberalism | Liberalism is a political ideology or worldview founded on ideas of liberty and equality. Liberals espouse a wide array of views depending on their understanding of these principles, but generally liberals support ideas such as constitutionalism, liberal democracy, free and fair elections, human rights and the free exercise of religion.

Liberalism first became a powerful force in the Age of Enlightenment, rejecting several foundational assumptions that dominated most earlier theories of government, such as nobility, established religion, absolute monarchy, and the Divine Right of Kings. |
|---|---|

1. _____ in politics is often seen as the midpoint in the three major political viewpoints of realism, _____, and internationalism. Whereas Realism and Internationalism are both on ends of the scale, _____ tends to occupy the middle ground on most issues, and finds compromise between these two conflicting points of view.

   Believers of _____ believe that multinational and multilateral organizations have their place in the world order, but not that a world government would be feasible.

   a. Rationalism
   b. Rationalist Society of Australia
   c. Rationalist-constructivist debate
   d. Sea of Faith

2. _____ describes a collection of views in philosophy which emphasize the context in which an action, utterance, or expression occurs, and argues that, in some important respect, the action, utterance, or expression can only be understood relative to that context. Contextualist views hold that philosophically controversial concepts, such as 'meaning P,' 'knowing that P,' 'having a reason to A,' and possibly even 'being true' or 'being right' only have meaning relative to a specified context. Some philosophers hold that context-dependence may lead to relativism; nevertheless, contextualist views are increasingly popular within philosophy.

   a. Definitionism
   b. Law of the infinite cornucopia
   c. Contextualism
   d. Proof

3. . The _____ was a cultural movement that spanned the period roughly from the 14th to the 17th century, beginning in Italy in the Late Middle Ages and later spreading to the rest of Europe. Though the invention of printing sped the dissemination of ideas from the later 15th century, the changes of the _____ were not uniformly experienced across Europe.

As a cultural movement, it encompassed innovative flowering of Latin and vernacular literatures, beginning with the 14th-century resurgence of learning based on classical sources, which contemporaries credited to Petrarch, the development of linear perspective and other techniques of rendering a more natural reality in painting, and gradual but widespread educational reform.

a. Renaissance humanism
b. Renaissance philosophy
c. Supposition theory
d. Renaissance

4. _____ is the view that the truth values of certain claims--especially claims about the existence or non-existence of any deity, but also other religious and metaphysical claims--are unknown or unknowable. _____ can be defined in various ways, and is sometimes used to indicate doubt or a skeptical approach to questions. In some senses, _____ is a stance about the difference between belief and knowledge, rather than about any specific claim or belief.

a. Amsterdam Declaration
b. Anti-clericalism
c. Antireligion
d. Agnosticism

5. The _____--in many traditional spiritual, philosophical, and psychological traditions--is the incorporeal and immortal essence of a person, living thing, or object. According to some religions (including the Abrahamic religions in most of their forms), _____s--or at least immortal _____s capable of union with the divine--belong only to human beings. For example, the Catholic theologian Thomas Aquinas attributed '_____' (anima) to all organisms but taught that only human _____s are immortal.

a. Transhumanism
b. Soul
c. Wali Kirani
d. Prophets of Islam

1. a
2. c
3. d
4. d
5. b

You can take the complete Chapter Practice Test

for 9. Faithful Re-readings: Exclusivism, Inclusivism, Pluralism, and Justice ...
on all key terms, persons, places, and concepts.

Online 99 Cents

http://www.JustTheFacts101.com

Use www.JustTheFacts101.com for all your study needs

including Facts101's online interactive problem solving labs in

chemistry, statistics, mathematics, and more.

10. Reflexive Re-readings: Looking at the Looker

CHAPTER OUTLINE: KEY TERMS, PEOPLE, PLACES, CONCEPTS

_____	Reflexivity
_____	Paranormal
_____	Religious experience
_____	Telepathy
_____	Ernst Bergmann
_____	Theology
_____	Mysticism
_____	Philosophical analysis
_____	Collective unconscious
_____	Humanities
_____	Poltergeist
_____	Psychology
_____	Rationalism
_____	Reductionism
_____	Skepticism
_____	Huston Cummings Smith
_____	Rabindranath Tagore
_____	Baul
_____	Plato
_____	Perception
_____	Sociology

10. Reflexive Re-readings: Looking at the Looker

CHAPTER OUTLINE: KEY TERMS, PEOPLE, PLACES, CONCEPTS

	Phenomenology
	Friedrich
	Gospel
	Criticism
	Historical criticism
	Miracles
	Suicide
	Theory
	Cicero
	Animal magnetism
	Clairvoyance
	Plotinus
	Near-death experience
	Reincarnation
	Magic
	Synchronicity
	Merton Thesis
	Animism
	Consciousness
	Panpsychism
	Tantra

10. Reflexive Re-readings: Looking at the Looker

	Yoga
	William Blake
	Spinoza
	Society
	Soul
	Richard Dawkins
	New Atheism
	Atheism
	Polemic
	Materialism

CHAPTER HIGHLIGHTS & NOTES: KEY TERMS, PEOPLE, PLACES, CONCEPTS

Reflexivity	Reflexivity refers to circular relationships between cause and effect. A reflexive relationship is bidirectional with both the cause and the effect affecting one another in a situation that does not render both functions causes and effects. In sociology, reflexivity therefore comes to mean an act of self-reference where examination or action 'bends back on', refers to, and affects the entity instigating the action or examination.
Paranormal	Paranormal is a general term that describes unusual experiences that supposedly lack a scientific explanation, or phenomena alleged to be outside of science's current ability to explain or measure. Notably, Paranormal phenomena also lack scientific evidence, as detectable but not well explained phenomena such as dark matter or dark energy are not commonly called Paranormal. In parapsychology, the term has, in the past, been used to describe the supposed phenomena of extra-sensory perception, including telepathy, and psychokinesis, ghosts, and hauntings.

Religious experience	A religious experience is a subjective experience in which an individual reports contact with a transcendent reality, an encounter or union with the divine. Such an experience often involves arriving at some knowledge or insight previously unavailable to the subject yet unnaccountable or unforseeable according to the usual conceptual or psychological framework within which the subject has been used to operating. Religious experience generally brings understanding, partial or complete, of issues of a fundamental character that may have been a cause (whether consciously ackowledged or not) of anguish or alienation to the subject for an extended period of time.
Telepathy	Telepathy , is the ostensible transfer of information on thoughts or feelings between individuals by means other than the five senses. The term was coined in 1882 by the classical scholar Fredric W. H. Myers, a founder of the Society for Psychical Research, specifically to replace the earlier expression thought-transference.
Ernst Bergmann	Ernst Bergmann (7 August 1881, Colditz, Kingdom of Saxony - 16 April 1945, Naumburg) was a German philosopher and proponent of Nazism. He studied philosophy and German philology at the University of Leipzig and got his PhD in 1905. Subsequently he continued his studies in Berlin. Later he returned to Leipzig, where he received the status of Privatdozent at the university in 1911. In 1916 he was awarded the position of Ausserordentlicher Professor (professor without chair).
Theology	Theology is the rational and systematic study of religion and its influences and of the nature of religious truth, or the learned profession acquired by specialized courses in religion, usually taught at a college or seminary. Augustine of Hippo defined the Latin equivalent, theologia, as 'reasoning or discussion concerning the Deity'; Richard Hooker defined 'theology' in English as 'the science of things divine'. The term can, however, be used for a variety of different disciplines or forms of discourse.
Mysticism	Mysticism is the pursuit of communion with, identity with divinity, spiritual truth intuition, instinct or insight. Mysticism usually centers on a practice or practices intended to nurture those experiences or awareness. Mysticism may be dualistic, maintaining a distinction between the self and the divine, or may be nondualistic.
Philosophical analysis	Philosophical analysis is a general term for techniques typically used by philosophers in the analytic tradition that involve 'breaking down' (i.e. analyzing) philosophical issues.
Collective unconscious	Collective unconscious is a term of analytical psychology, coined by Carl Jung. It is proposed to be a part of the unconscious mind, expressed in humanity and all life forms with nervous systems, and describes how the structure of the psyche autonomously organizes experience.

10. Reflexive Re-readings: Looking at the Looker

Humanities	The humanities are academic disciplines that study the human condition, using methods that are primarily analytical, critical, or speculative, as distinguished from the mainly empirical approaches of the natural sciences.
	The humanities include ancient and modern languages, literature, history, philosophy, religion, and visual and performing arts such as music and theatre. The humanities that are also regarded as social sciences include technology, history, anthropology, area studies, communication studies, cultural studies, law and linguistics.
Poltergeist	In folklore and the paranormal, a poltergeist is the apparent manifestation of an imperceptible but noisy, disruptive or destructive entity. Most accounts of poltergeist manifestations involve noises and destruction that have no apparent cause. Reports also include inanimate objects being picked up and thrown as if by an invisible person; noises such as knocking, rapping, or even human voices; and petty physical attacks on human beings, such as pinching, biting, and hitting.
Psychology	Psychology is an academic and applied discipline that involves the scientific study of mental functions and behaviors. Psychology has the immediate goal of understanding individuals and groups by both establishing general principles and researching specific cases, and by many accounts it ultimately aims to benefit society. In this field, a professional practitioner or researcher is called a psychologist and can be classified as a social, behavioral, or cognitive scientist.
Rationalism	Rationalism in politics is often seen as the midpoint in the three major political viewpoints of realism, rationalism, and internationalism. Whereas Realism and Internationalism are both on ends of the scale, rationalism tends to occupy the middle ground on most issues, and finds compromise between these two conflicting points of view.
	Believers of Rationalism believe that multinational and multilateral organizations have their place in the world order, but not that a world government would be feasible.
Reductionism	Reductionism can mean either (a) an approach to understanding the nature of complex things by reducing them to the interactions of their parts, or to simpler or more fundamental things or (b) a philosophical position that a complex system is nothing but the sum of its parts, and that an account of it can be reduced to accounts of individual constituents. This can be said of objects, phenomena, explanations, theories, and meanings.
	Reductionism strongly reflects a certain perspective on causality.
Skepticism	Skepticism, but generally refers to any questioning attitude towards knowledge, facts, or opinions/beliefs stated as facts, or doubt regarding claims that are taken for granted elsewhere.

	The word may characterize a position on a single matter, as in the case of religious skepticism, which is 'doubt concerning basic religious principles (such as immortality, providence, and revelation)', but philosophical skepticism is an overall approach that requires all information to be well supported by evidence. Skeptics may even doubt the reliability of their own senses.
Huston Cummings Smith	Huston Cummings Smith is a religious studies scholar in the United States. His book The World's Religions, remains a popular introduction to comparative religion. Smith was born in Soochow, China to Methodist missionaries and spent his first 17 years there.
Rabindranath Tagore	Rabindranath Tagore was an Indian Bengali polymath. He was a popular poet, novelist, musician, and playwright who reshaped Bengali literature and music in the late 19th and early 20th centuries. As author of Gitanjali and its 'profoundly sensitive, fresh and beautiful verse', and as the first Asian to win the Nobel Prize in Literature, Rabindranath Tagore was perhaps the most widely regarded Indian literary figure of all time.
Baul	Baul are a group of mystic minstrels from Bengal. Bauls constitute both a syncretic religious sect and a musical tradition. Bauls are a very heterogeneous group, with many sects, but their membership mainly consists of Vaishnava Hindus and Sufi Muslims.
Plato	Plato was a Classical Greek philosopher, mathematician, student of Socrates, writer of philosophical dialogues, and founder of the Academy in Athens, the first institution of higher learning in the Western world. Along with his mentor, Socrates, and his student, Aristotle, Plato helped to lay the foundations of Western philosophy and science. In the words of A. N. Whitehead:' The safest general characterization of the European philosophical tradition is that it consists of a series of footnotes to Plato.'
Perception	Perception is the organization, identification, and interpretation of sensory information in order to fabricate a mental representation through the process of transduction, which sensors in the body transform signals from the environment into encoded neural signals. All perception involves signals in the nervous system, which in turn result from physical stimulation of the sense organs. For example, vision involves light striking the retinas of the eyes, smell is mediated by odor molecules and hearing involves pressure waves.
Sociology	Sociology is the study of human social behavior and its origins, development, organizations, and institutions. It is a social science which uses various methods of empirical investigation and critical analysis to develop a body of knowledge about human social actions, social structure and functions. A goal for many sociologists is to conduct research which may be applied directly to social policy and welfare, while others focus primarily on refining the theoretical understanding of social processes.

10. Reflexive Re-readings: Looking at the Looker

Phenomenology	The term phenomenology in science is used to describe a body of knowledge that relates empirical observations of phenomena to each other, in a way that is consistent with fundamental theory, but is not directly derived from theory. For example, we find the following definition in the Concise Dictionary of Physics:' Phenomenological Theory. A theory that expresses mathematically the results of observed phenomena without paying detailed attention to their fundamental significance.'
Friedrich	The Friedrich are the most ancient German-Bohemian glass-maker family. History From as early as 750 years ago, the shadowy picture of the oldest German-Bohemian glass-maker family Friedrich emerges, who contributed greatly towards the creation of the world-famous Bohemian glass (also called Bohemian Crystal). In pre-Hussite times they produced amazing works of vitreous art near Daubitz, nowadays called Doubice.
Gospel	A Gospel is a writing that describes the life of Jesus. The word is primarily used to refer to the four canonical Gospels: the Gospel of Matthew, Gospel of Mark, Gospel of Luke and Gospel of John, probably written between AD 65 and 80. They appear to have been originally untitled; they were quoted anonymously in the first half of the second century (i.e. 100-150) but the names by which they are currently known appear suddenly around the year 180. The first canonical Gospel written is thought by most scholars to be Mark (c 65-70), which was according to the majority used as a source for the Gospels of Matthew and Luke.
Criticism	Criticism is the practice of judging the merits and faults of something or someone in an intelligible (or articulate) way. •The judger is called 'the critic'.•To engage in criticism is 'to criticize'.•One specific item of criticism is called 'a criticism'. Criticism can be:•directed toward a person or an animal; at a group, authority or organization; at a specific behaviour; or at an object of some kind (an idea, a relationship, a condition, a process, or a thing).•personal (delivered directly from one person to another, in a personal capacity), or impersonal (expressing the view of an organization, and not aimed at anyone personally).•highly specific and detailed, or very abstract and general.•verbal (expressed in language) or non-verbal (expressed symbolically, or expressed through an action or a way of behaving).•explicit (the criticism is clearly stated) or implicit (a criticism is implied by what is being said, but it is not stated openly).•the result of critical thinking or spontaneous impulse. To criticize does not necessarily imply 'to find fault', but the word is often taken to mean the simple expression of an objection against prejudice, or a disapproval.

Historical criticism	Historical criticism, is a branch of literary criticism that investigates the origins of ancient text in order to understand 'the world behind the text'.
	The primary goal of historical criticism is to ascertain the text's primitive or original meaning in its original historical context and its literal sense or sensus literalis historicus. The secondary goal seeks to establish a reconstruction of the historical situation of the author and recipients of the text.
Miracles	Thomas Paine, one of the Founding Fathers of the American Revolution, wrote 'All the tales of Miracles with which the Old and New Testament are filled, are fit only for impostors to preach and fools to believe'.
	Thomas Jefferson, principle author of the Declaration of Independence, edited a version of the Bible in which he removed sections of the New Testament containing supernatural aspects as well as perceived misinterpretations he believed had been added by the Four Evangelists. Jefferson wrote, 'The establishment of the innocent and genuine character of this benevolent moralist, and the rescuing it from the imputation of imposture, which has resulted from artificial systems, [footnote: e.g. The immaculate conception of Jesus, his deification, the creation of the world by him, his miraculous powers, his resurrection and visible ascension, his corporeal presence in the Eucharist, the Trinity; original sin, atonement, regeneration, election, orders of Hierarchy, etc.
Suicide	Suicide is the act of intentionally causing one's own death. Suicide is often committed out of despair, the cause of which is frequently attributed to a mental disorder such as depression, bipolar disorder, schizophrenia, alcoholism, or drug abuse. Stress factors such as financial difficulties or troubles with interpersonal relationships often play a role.
Theory	In mathematical logic, a theory (also called a formal theory) is a set of sentences in a formal language. Usually a deductive system is understood from context. An element $\phi \in T$ of a theory T is then called an axiom of the theory, and any sentence that follows from the axioms ($T \vdash \phi$) is called a theorem of the theory.
Cicero	Marcus Tullius Cicero was a Roman philosopher, statesman, lawyer, orator, political theorist, Roman consul and constitutionalist. He came from a wealthy municipal family of the equestrian order, and is widely considered one of Rome's greatest orators and prose stylists.
	He introduced the Romans to the chief schools of Greek philosophy and created a Latin philosophical vocabulary (with neologisms such as humanitas, qualitas, quantitas, and essentia) distinguishing himself as a linguist, translator, and philosopher.

10. Reflexive Re-readings: Looking at the Looker

Animal magnetism	Animal magnetism is a term proposed by Franz Mesmer in the 18th century, the term 'magnetism' was adopted by analogy, referring to some interpersonal and general effects of reciprocal influence and/or entanglement he observed. Mesmer attributed such effects to a supposed 'life energy' or 'fluid' or ethereal medium believed to reside in the bodies of animate beings (i.e., those who breathe). The term is translated from Mesmer's magnétisme animal.
Clairvoyance	The term Clairvoyance is used to refer to the ability to gain information about an object, person, location or physical event through means other than the known human senses, a form of extra-sensory perception. A person said to have the ability of Clairvoyance is referred to as a clairvoyant .
	Claims for the existence of paranormal and psychic abilities such as Clairvoyance are highly controversial.
Plotinus	Plotinus was a major philosopher of the ancient world. In his system of theory there are the three principles: the One, the Intellect, and the Soul. His teacher was Ammonius Saccas and he is of the Platonic tradition.
Near-death experience	A near-death experience refers to a broad range of personal experiences associated with impending death, encompassing multiple possible sensations including detachment from the body; feelings of levitation; extreme fear; total serenity, security, or warmth; the experience of absolute dissolution; and the presence of a light.
	These phenomena are usually reported after an individual has been clinically dead or otherwise very close to death, hence the term near-death experience. Many NDE reports, however, originate from events that are not life-threatening.
Reincarnation	Reincarnation is a 2008 fantasy novel by American author Suzanne Weyn. The novel was released on January 1, 2008. It tells the story of a two lovers who attempt to find each other through the centuries. The narrative follows the action through time.
Magic	Magic (sometimes referred to as stage magic to distinguish it from paranormal or ritual magic) is a performing art that entertains audiences by staging tricks or creating illusions of seemingly impossible or supernatural feats using natural means. These feats are called magic tricks, effects, or illusions.
	One who performs such illusions is called a magician or an illusionist.
Synchronicity	Synchronicity is the experience of two or more events that are apparently causally unrelated or unlikely to occur together by chance, yet are experienced as occurring together in a meaningful manner. The concept of synchronicity was first described in this terminology by Carl Gustav Jung, a Swiss psychologist, in the 1920s.

Merton Thesis	The Merton Thesis is an argument about the nature of early experimental science proposed by Robert K. Merton. Similar to Max Weber's famous claim on the link between Protestant ethic and the capitalist economy, Merton argued for a similar positive correlation between the rise of Protestant pietism and early experimental science. The Merton Thesis has resulted in continuous debates.
Animism	Animism is a philosophical, religious or spiritual idea that souls or spirits exist not only in humans but also in other animals, plants, rocks, natural phenomena such as thunder, geographic features such as mountains or rivers a proposition also known as hylozoism in philosophy. Animism may further attribute souls to abstract concepts such as words, true names or metaphors in mythology. Religions which emphasize Animism are mostly folk religions, such as the various forms of Shamanism, but also Shinto and certain currents of Hinduism emphasize the concept.
Consciousness	Consciousness is the quality or state of being aware of an external object or something within oneself. It has been defined as: subjectivity, awareness, the ability to experience or to feel, wakefulness, having a sense of selfhood, and the executive control system of the mind. Despite the difficulty in definition, many philosophers believe that there is a broadly shared underlying intuition about what consciousness is.
Panpsychism	In philosophy, panpsychism is the view that all matter has a mental aspect, or, alternatively, all objects have a unified center of experience or point of view. Baruch Spinoza, Gottfried Leibniz, Gustav Theodor Fechner, Friedrich Paulsen, Ernst Haeckel, Charles Strong, and partially William James are considered panpsychists.

Panexperientialism, as espoused by Alfred North Whitehead, is a less bold variation, which credits all entities with phenomenal consciousness but not with cognition, and therefore not necessarily with full-fledged minds. |
Tantra	Tantra and the universe is regarded as the divine play of Shakti and Shiva. The word Tantra also applies to any of the scriptures (called 'Tantras') commonly identified with the worship of Shakti. Tantra deals primarily with spiritual practices and ritual forms of worship, which aim at liberation from ignorance and rebirth.
Yoga	Yoga refers to traditional physical and mental disciplines that originated in India. The word is associated with meditative practices in Hinduism, Buddhism and Jainism. Within Hinduism, it refers to one of the six orthodox (astika) schools of Hindu philosophy, and to the goal towards which that school directs its practices.
William Blake	William Blake (28 November 1757 - 12 August 1827) was an English poet, painter, and printmaker. Largely unrecognised during his lifetime, Blake is now considered a seminal figure in the history of both the poetry and visual arts of the Romantic Age.

10. Reflexive Re-readings: Looking at the Looker

Spinoza	Baruch or Benedict de Spinoza was a Dutch philosopher of Portuguese Jewish origin. Revealing considerable scientific aptitude, the breadth and importance of Spinoza's work was not fully realized until years after his death. Today, he is considered one of the great rationalists of 17th-century philosophy, laying the groundwork for the 18th century Enlightenment and modern biblical criticism.
Society	A society, or a human society, is a group of people involved with each other through persistent relations, or a large social grouping sharing the same geographical or social territory, subject to the same political authority and dominant cultural expectations. Human societies are characterized by patterns of relationships (social relations) between individuals who share a distinctive culture and institutions; a given society may be described as the sum total of such relationships among its constituent members. In the social sciences, a larger society often evinces stratification and/or dominance patterns in subgroups.
Soul	The soul--in many traditional spiritual, philosophical, and psychological traditions--is the incorporeal and immortal essence of a person, living thing, or object. According to some religions (including the Abrahamic religions in most of their forms), souls--or at least immortal souls capable of union with the divine--belong only to human beings. For example, the Catholic theologian Thomas Aquinas attributed 'soul' (anima) to all organisms but taught that only human souls are immortal.
Richard Dawkins	Clinton Richard Dawkins, FRS, FRSL is a British ethologist, evolutionary biologist and popular science author. He was formerly Professor for Public Understanding of Science at Oxford and was a fellow of New College, Oxford. Dawkins came to prominence with his 1976 book The Selfish Gene, which popularised the gene-centred view of evolution and introduced the term meme.
New Atheism	New Atheism is the name given to the ideas promoted by a collection of 21st-century atheist writers who have advocated the view that 'religion should not simply be tolerated but should be countered, criticized, and exposed by rational argument wherever its influence arises.' The term is commonly associated with individuals such as Richard Dawkins, Daniel Dennett, Sam Harris, and the late Christopher Hitchens (together called 'the Four Horsemen of New Atheism' in a 2007 debate they held on their criticisms of religion, a name that has stuck) and Victor J. Stenger. Several best-selling books by these authors, published between 2004 and 2007, form the basis for much of the discussion of new atheism. History The 2004 publication of The End of Faith: Religion, Terror, and the Future of Reason by Sam Harris, a bestseller in the USA, marked the first of a series of popular bestsellers.
Atheism	Atheism is, in a broad sense, the rejection of belief in the existence of deities. In a narrower sense, atheism is specifically the position that there are no deities.

Polemic	A polemic is a contentious argument that is intended to establish the truth of a specific belief and the falsity of the contrary belief. Polemics are mostly seen in arguments about very controversial topics.
	The art or practice of such argumentation is called polemics.
Materialism	In philosophy, the theory of materialism holds that the only thing that exists is matter or energy; that all things are composed of material and all phenomena (including consciousness) are the result of material interactions. In other words, matter is the only substance, and reality is identical with the actually occurring states of energy and matter.
	To many philosophers, 'materialism' is synonymous with 'physicalism'.

1. _____ is a general term for techniques typically used by philosophers in the analytic tradition that involve 'breaking down' (i.e. analyzing) philosophical issues.

    a. Racing thoughts
    b. Synectics
    c. Philosophical analysis
    d. Credo ut intelligam

2. In philosophy, _____ is the view that all matter has a mental aspect, or, alternatively, all objects have a unified center of experience or point of view. Baruch Spinoza, Gottfried Leibniz, Gustav Theodor Fechner, Friedrich Paulsen, Ernst Haeckel, Charles Strong, and partially William James are considered panpsychists.

    Panexperientialism, as espoused by Alfred North Whitehead, is a less bold variation, which credits all entities with phenomenal consciousness but not with cognition, and therefore not necessarily with full-fledged minds.

    a. Phenomenalism
    b. Panpsychism
    c. Property dualism
    d. Psychological egoism

3. . _____ refers to circular relationships between cause and effect. A reflexive relationship is bidirectional with both the cause and the effect affecting one another in a situation that does not render both functions causes and effects. In sociology, _____ therefore comes to mean an act of self-reference where examination or action 'bends back on', refers to, and affects the entity instigating the action or examination.

a. Reflexivity
b. Resource mobilization
c. Reverse psychology
d. Rule complex

4. A _____ is a writing that describes the life of Jesus. The word is primarily used to refer to the four canonical _____s: the _____ of Matthew, _____ of Mark, _____ of Luke and _____ of John, probably written between AD 65 and 80. They appear to have been originally untitled; they were quoted anonymously in the first half of the second century (i.e. 100-150) but the names by which they are currently known appear suddenly around the year 180.

The first canonical _____ written is thought by most scholars to be Mark (c 65-70), which was according to the majority used as a source for the _____s of Matthew and Luke.

a. Gospel
b. Frida Kahlo
c. Ban Chao
d. Stephen William Hawking

5. Thomas Paine, one of the Founding Fathers of the American Revolution, wrote 'All the tales of _____ with which the Old and New Testament are filled, are fit only for impostors to preach and fools to believe'.

Thomas Jefferson, principle author of the Declaration of Independence, edited a version of the Bible in which he removed sections of the New Testament containing supernatural aspects as well as perceived misinterpretations he believed had been added by the Four Evangelists. Jefferson wrote, 'The establishment of the innocent and genuine character of this benevolent moralist, and the rescuing it from the imputation of imposture, which has resulted from artificial systems, [footnote: e.g. The immaculate conception of Jesus, his deification, the creation of the world by him, his miraculous powers, his resurrection and visible ascension, his corporeal presence in the Eucharist, the Trinity; original sin, atonement, regeneration, election, orders of Hierarchy, etc.

a. Secular humanism
b. Christian humanism
c. Religious humanism
d. Miracles

1. c
2. b
3. a
4. a
5. d

You can take the complete Chapter Practice Test

for 10. Reflexive Re-readings: Looking at the Looker
on all key terms, persons, places, and concepts.

Online 99 Cents

http://www.JustTheFacts101.com

Use www.JustTheFacts101.com for all your study needs

including Facts101's online interactive problem solving labs in

chemistry, statistics, mathematics, and more.

Want More?
JustTheFacts101.com...

Jtf101.com provides the outlines and highlights of your textbooks, just like this e-StudyGuide, but also gives you the PRACTICE TESTS, and other exclusive study tools for all of your textbooks.

Learn More. *Just click*
http://www.JustTheFacts101.com/

CPSIA information can be obtained
at www.ICGtesting.com
Printed in the USA
FSOW02n1257290116
16355FS